To Mum

Happy Mothers Day 19[...]

Lots of love,

Ray
+ Terry
x x x

To Mum
Happy Mothers Day 19[...]

Geoffrey Smith's
World of Flowers

Edited by Brian Davies

PEERAGE BOOKS

Published to accompany the BBC television series
Geoffrey Smith's World of Flowers
First broadcast on BBC2 in 1983 and 1984

Produced by Brian Davies

The programmes were prepared in consultation with
the BBC Continuing Education Advisory Council

All the colour photographs in this book were specially
taken for the BBC by Mel Davies, with the exception
of those provided by Pat Brindley on pages 24, 25 (top)
and 60, and Ian Butterfield on page 87 (top left)

First published in this format in Great Britain in 1984 by
the British Broadcasting Corporation

This edition published in 1988 by
Peerage Books
Michelin House
81 Fulham Road
London SW3 6RB

Reprinted 1989

Copyright © Geoffrey Smith and the
British Broadcasting Corporation 1983 and 1984

ISBN 1 85052 112 3

Printed in Czechoslovakia
50676/2

Above:
Narcissus pseudonarcissus happily naturalised in a woodland setting at the Savill gardens

Title page:
Geoffrey Smith finds *Cypripedium calceolus*, the 'Lady Slipper' orchid, in the Swiss Alps

Half title:
Fuchsia 'Snowcap'

Contents

Introduction

Plants, fortunately, pay no heed to international boundaries. *Lilium pardalinum*, the leopard lily, growing wild in the giant redwood forests in California, will accept, without obvious discomfort, being transplanted to a woodland in England. *Pelargonium peltatum*, the ivy-leaved geranium, growing on a South African hillside, may be seen covering a twelve feet high bush in thousands of flowers. It is our good fortune that the long trailing stems of *Pelargonium peltatum*, weaving themselves up through the thorn bush on that wild sun-baked hillside, flower with the same freedom when cascading from a window box in Wapping.

Many of the plants in this book and the series of programmes made for BBC television were introduced to gardens centuries ago; others are comparative newcomers. All, without exception, carry with them a thread of human history. Plant hunters, explorers, traders, pioneers, wealthy amateur botanists on sight-seeing expeditions, and indeed people from almost every walk of life assisted in the discovery and introduction of so many of the well-loved plants which grace our gardens today. The countries of the world supplied the material; human curiosity and courage provided the means; while gardeners subscribe the accolade of appreciation.

I am most indebted to Elizabeth Farrar, Peter Barnes, Sabina Knees and Bettina Wilkes who had the unenviable task of checking the manuscript, thus helping me to avoid the major pitfalls of plant nomenclature.

My thanks to Mel Davies whose superb pictures make each page a garden. Also to Frank Holland whose application and patience throughout on the design of the book make even the most avid gardener seem impetuous by comparison.

Finally, my grateful thanks to all the people who allowed us access to their gardens to photograph the flowers.

Right:
The author at the home of *Lilium* 'Enchantment' in Oregon

I
Alpines

An alpine, so far as the gardener is concerned, includes any plant capable of being cultivated in a rock garden, scree bed, or alpine house without looking incongruous. In botanical terms, the definition is more exact. Alpines are those plants which grow in extremes of climate where the growing season is curtailed – as, for example, in Arctic tundra, or above the tree line in mountainous regions of the world. The altitude at which plant life survives varies from sea level on the Arctic fringe to many thousands of feet above sea level in the Alps or Himalayas. With such a wide geographical range the variations in soil and habitat are enormous. A soil-packed crevice on a south-facing cliff in the Dolomites is vastly different from the conditions of soil and weather which exist in the peat bogs of the tundra. A plant growing in an exposed rock face must be capable of enduring months of sub-zero temperatures with no protecting cover of snow. In summer, hot sunlight reflecting from the bare rock has a dehydrating effect which would desiccate any but the most specialised plant. Screes and moraines, the great jumbled masses of stone which tumble down the mountain sides, are also colonised by plants. The stone slides are formed by the weathering of the bare rock. Extremes of heat and cold with constant attack from wind and rain slowly break down the solid rock. The broken fragments roll down the steep slope, eventually finding their angle of rest and stability. The stones composing the moraine or scree are of various sizes, from boulders weighing many tons to fine sand mixed with plant remains and forming a very quick drainage system for roots. This is compensated for in some degree by the mineral-rich moisture which percolates down through them from the melting snow above. Like the plants growing on the exposed rock face, those of scree or moraine have widely spread root systems which tap the underground water to support only a small amount of top growth. This is a feature of many high alpine plants: widely ramifying roots and small leaves providing only the minimum area to the dehydrating effects of sun and wind.

Moderately level plateaux where a depth of humus-rich soil has accumulated support a plant community that is less specialised but equally interesting from the gardener's point of view.

A meadow in the Swiss Alps

Indeed, this is the fascination of alpines – charming the eye with their beauty while challenging skill in cultivation.

Naturally, mountains composed of Dolomitic limestone are inhabited by a different plant community from that found on mountains which offer a neutral or acid soil. Fortunately, even in a small area the alpine enthusiast can provide the different soil conditions which suit a saxifraga from the Dolomites or a gentian from the Himalayas, all in the space of a few feet.

Considering the extremes of climate, exposure, and the immense variation in soil composition and chemistry, the type of plant life collectively described as 'alpines' is not surprising. What never fails to astonish me is how readily so many alpines will adapt to conditions in lowland gardens. That they do so while still retaining the charm, beauty of flower or foliage and compactness of growth which attracts gardeners in the first place is our good fortune. There are exceptions which, on being transferred to the lusher, less vigorous environment of the garden, do lose character. They grow coarse, fail to flower, and in general behave like a noxious weed. Others are incapable of making the change, trapped by the defensive mechanisms which enable them to survive alpine conditions. The felted or hairy foliage, a barrier to cold or sun at high elevations, traps moisture at lower altitudes.

Alpine plants are accustomed to clearly defined seasons with winter an unbroken dormant period. In the garden warm sunshine following frost persuades a plant winter is over, then a further burst of cold weather catches it in full growth. To counteract the worst effects which a change of climate and soil produces, the gardener should make the best provision possible. A porous, well-drained soil is essential, supplied with moisture throughout the growing season, yet not liable to waterlogging in winter. Although alpines do not as a rule need shelter from frost, some, however, do need protection from the constant dampness of lowland winters.

A well-constructed alpine house will give adequate protection to any plants which are seriously harmed by being too wet for long periods during the winter. An alpine house needs to be purpose built. Ventilators along the full length on both sides of the ridge, and side ventilation with additional louvre-style vents in the wall below staging level are, if not essential, extremely valuable. Mass-produced, general-purpose greenhouses are capable of being converted into an alpine house by the install-ation of a fan or air circulator as an aid to the existing ventilation system. Just to see the mountain plants which in a greenhouse flower in January, petals unspoilt by the weather, is complete justification for any indulgence necessary to ensure their good health.

Over the last thirty years I have constructed rock gardens using limestone, millstone grit, sandstone and tufa. They ranged in size from well over an acre to a modest little outcrop 6 feet by 8 feet (1·8 m by 2·4 m) in the middle of a lawn. Each time I have taken great care to ensure that the stones were laid in such a way as to reproduce the appearance of a natural rock formation. Certainly, after years of building, then maintaining rock gardens, the only advantage to accrue from all the labour was that the plants were presented in a 'natural' setting. Few things look more unnatural than a limestone outcrop in a suburban garden surrounded by carefully squared and trimmed hedges. Good-quality stone is extremely expensive and heavy to handle.

Bearing in mind the main essentials for the successful cultiva-tion of alpines, good drainage, free air circulation, and full light can all be supplied by table beds which are raised a little above the general level of the garden, then filled with compost specially prepared to suit a plant's requirements. The bed, which can be constructed to any shape required in brick or stone, once established is pleasantly easy to weed and top dress. Hollow walls with a brick, stone, or breeze-block outer skin and the centre

filled with soil offer just the conditions which even some of the more demanding alpines find congenial. Of all the suggestions made for the cultivation of alpines, possibly a scree bed works best in practice. Construction is simple although a little laborious. On a sloping site simply dig out the soil to a depth of 20 to 24 inches (51 to 61 cm). Keep the top soil separate and dispose of the sub-soil elsewhere in the garden. I spread several dozen barrowloads thinly over the vegetable garden, then mix it in while winter digging. The next step is to lay a 10- to 12-inch (25- to 30-cm) layer of broken stone in the excavation to provide drainage. On top of this is spread a layer of half-rotted leaves, coarse peat, or reversed turf – anything which prevents the fine compost from the top layer washing down into the drainage holes between the stones. The final stage is to mix the excavated top soil with stone chips, very sharp sand, plus a little peat as a moisture holder.

Aim at producing a very gritty, free-draining top 12 inches (30 cm) to the scree. This is a general-purpose mixture to suit the less demanding alpines. Pockets can be made with peat for those plants requiring more moisture; conversely, extra grit can be added as required for those plants which thrive in poorer conditions. Whether the choice of the construction falls on the traditional rock garden, scree, table bed, hollow wall, or just raking sand on to a sloping site in the garden, it will need supplementary care once the plants are established: weeding, watering in dry weather, then feeding and top dressing with freshly mixed compost to maintain the rooting medium in good condition. To anyone who thinks this is a lot of work and trouble just to grow alpines, I would say they are the most fascinating, diverse, yet at the same time exasperating of all the plants I have ever grown. From *Gentiana verna*, which grows in Teesdale, to the *celmisia* from New Zealand, they possess a charm which I find irresistible.

The specialist who desires to know more and more about less and less will find satisfaction in studying a single genus containing a large number of species. Campanula or saxifraga are examples of these. At the risk of suffering severe horticultural

Above and left: *Gentiana verna* growing wild in the French Alps

Right: *Pulsatilla alpina*

indigestion I grow any of the mountain flowers available that attract me, and have not yet done more than discover what a wealth of beautiful plants there are.

The European mountains, which support several hundred species of garden worth, are sufficiently accessible for the enthusiast actually to go and see the plants growing naturally. There in an alpine meadow with snow-capped mountains beyond may be seen *Pulsatilla alpina*, *Saxifraga oppositifolia* and *Gentiana verna* forming a dark red and blue fringe to the clear water of an alpine lake. Alternatively, at the end of the day after a surfeit of flowers, one can wade through meadows of *Lilium martagon*. These are moments to recapture annually as the same plants grow to flower in your own garden.

For those who garden a soil which is naturally alkaline, before deciding whether to build a rock garden, table bed, or scree, it is my experience that only in a table bed is it easy to provide and maintain the acid, lime-free soil which is necessary to grow certain calcifuge (lime-hating) plants. With a suitable home prepared and ready, the most pleasant task of all is choosing those plants which will form a basis of our alpine collection. *Do not* under any circumstances go and dig up wild plants. All other considerations apart, in most countries now this is illegal. Look at the plants, then buy those selected from one of the many nurseries that specialise in alpines.

Many, even the choicest, can be grown from seed – the method I prefer. The shortest route to an intimate understanding of a plant's needs is to tend it from seed packet to maturity. One special lesson that all would-be growers of mountain plants should learn is that rarity is no guarantee of beauty. Familiar, easy-to-grow plants which flourish in gardens all over the country would not be so popular if they were not good value. An example of this universal popularity is *Alyssum saxatile* from Eastern Europe, where it inhabits rocks and similar stony places. The leaves are grey-green and the flowers, which open during April and May, are a deep golden yellow. As would be expected with a plant which has been grown in British gardens for close on three hundred years, there are many named clonal forms: 'Citrinum' with yellow flowers; 'Dudley Neville' with buff orange flowers; and 'Plenum' which, as the name implies, is full double. Commonly seen in spring bedding, alyssum looks handsome as an edge to a rock garden, table bed, or hollow wall.

Of equal merit and widely cultivated is aubrieta, which grows in the wild from Iran to Sicily. The most important species in gardening terms is *Aubrieta deltoidea*, parent of so many garden forms. Few plants flower with greater freedom in spring, given a place in lime soil and full sun. They should be trimmed hard back after flowering to keep top growth neat. Named varieties or good coloured forms are best increased by cuttings or division. They make good carpeting plants, and look superb growing in a wall or rock crevice in association with alyssum.

Androsace enjoys a fairly wide distribution throughout Europe and Asia. I am familiar with several of these species, but have never succeeded with any from very high altitudes. Some

Above: *Saxifraga oppositifolia* 'Splendens' in a table bed
Below: A garden form of *Sempervivum tectorum* growing in a limestone scree bed

Androsace vandellii

are easy to grow if provided with a scree-type soil, others, from high up rock faces in the mountains, will not thrive outdoors in this country, and are better accommodated in a frame or alpine house. Undoubtedly, those I have grown are amongst the most attractive mountain flowers to have graced my garden. I first saw *Androsace alpina* growing 13 000 feet (4 000 m) up a scree on the Pointe des Lessières in the Val d'Isère in the French Alps. It has soft, hairy leaves covered in bright pink flowers. Only in its natural habitat does this gem so reward: in the garden it is what can best be described as a reluctant participant. Of equal charm, *A. vandellii* is more compliant, at least if grown in a gritty mixture in an alpine house. The dense cushion of grey felted leaves and myriads of white flowers, each with a yellow eye, is breath-takingly beautiful. The plants I found were growing in a vertical crevice across the face of a cliff 300 feet (91 m) high in the Alps. I grew stock from seed which flowered for three springs in the alpine house; I just never dare risk growing them in the open garden. This is part of the fascination which alpines have for me; even within a single genus there are species so difficult to grow that sometimes the specialists are driven to despair. As if to compensate, there are others so delightfully easy to accommodate that they flatter our gardening ego. *A. primuloides* from the Himalayas is singularly obliging in this respect. Planted in a gritty scree sloping south, the rosettes of silver-haired leaves

push up 6-inch (15-cm) high stems, topped with clusters of deep pink flowers.

Aquilegia alpina

Even the aquilegia, normally so easy to grow, offers one or two temperamental high mountain forms. Most are no problem, except that they cross-pollinate with such liberal promiscuity that it is difficult to tell the legitimate from the illegitimate. So far I have never seen an ugly aquilegia. *Aquilegia alpina*, which I discovered growing wild in the Alps near Mont Cenis, has large blue and white flowers and grows about 12 inches (30 cm) high. Unfortunately, the only way to keep the true species is not to grow any other aquilegia within half a mile. *A. bertolonii*, at around 4 inches (10 cm) tall with bright blue flowers, is a gem best accommodated in a scree or hollow wall.

A. discolor is the species which gives me most pleasure. Dwarf in stature at 4 to 6 inches (10 to 15 cm) high with blue and white flowers over grey-green foliage, it is lovely, and easy to grow in most soils.

So often a large genus promises much yet gives little, and this is my experience with aster. Only one species measured up for cultivation in the rock garden, the European *Aster alpinus*. The tufted narrow leaves and large, purple, golden-centred daisy flowers on 6-inch (15-cm) stems are a feature in my limestone rock garden. There may be other good alpine species which so far I have not discovered.

Campanula allionii

The sun-loving campanula, popularly known as the 'Bell flower', offers so large a selection of species suitable for the rock garden that I am spoiled for choice. *Campanula allionii* from the European Alps grows best in a scree where it can spread by underground stems safe from marauding slugs. The large purple flowers open on stems which are only 3 inches (7 cm) high. The best-known is *C. carpatica* from the Bucegi mountains in the Transylvanian Alps of south-central Romania. It grows well in most soils and flowers profusely. I prefer named forms which grow no more than 6 inches (15 cm) high. The pick of the lot is *C. turbinata,* with dark blue, upturned bells carried one to a stem.

Cypripedium calceolus

Crocus vernus albiflorus

Again, as the slugs devour it avidly, the least vulnerable place is in a scree bed or hollow wall. Two plants of *C. cochleariifolia* have graced the hollow wall in front of my house for the last four years. The two have spread decorously by underground stems so that the white and blue colour forms intermingle. Then in June each year the bright green leaves are hidden by dancing legions of thimble-like bells on 2-inch (5-cm) stems. Only once have I seen the plant growing wild; it was in Austria where the flowers were less numerous but the back-cloth of the mountains was much more spectacular.

Crocus is so much a part of the spring scene – and then again of the autumn – that it would be difficult not to mention them if only briefly. *Crocus albiflorus* frequents the high alpine pastures from France to Yugoslavia. The flowers, white-flushed with blue, appear as the snow melts. The best-known of all the species crocus, *C. chrysanthus*, parent of so many hybrids, is a much better garden plant. Grow the corms in a well-drained soil in full sun. For further interest I raise fresh stock from seed, which takes three or four years from sowing to flowering.

For the autumn *C. speciosus* is the easiest to grow, even naturalising if planted in short, cropped turf. Its flowers are deep lilac blue.

Many cyclamen are not reliably hardy and must be grown indoors. *Cyclamen coum*, which comes from Eastern Europe, flowers in winter and spring in the garden and is perfectly hardy. The leaves of my plants are kidney-shaped, dark green above, red underneath. The shorter-petalled flowers on 2-inch (5-cm) stems are deep crimson or pink.

C. hederifolium is a great coloniser when suited by soil and situation. The leaves, beautifully marbled cream on green, are a feature right through the winter, and the large pink flowers open in the autumn before the leaves. Partial shade and a leaf-mould soil suit my plants satisfactorily.

I found the 'Lady Slipper' orchid, *Cypripedium calceolus*, growing in a boulder-strewn valley just on the edge of woodland in the Swiss Alps. To me it represents everything that I desire of a true alpine plant.

My first meeting with *Daphne cneorum* was in the Alps, on the Col d'Izoard, above the Durance valley, where it was growing in open glades, the fragrant pink flowers closely packed in terminal clusters only just protruding above the grass. The shrub grows in my rock garden with an annual top dressing of leaf mould, and it flowers in May. *D. striata* is similar, and grows in pockets of peat in stabilised scree at Lautaret. This species is not at all easy to cultivate in gardens, unlike *D. cneorum*.

Dianthus is an integral part of the summer garden scene, so it is fortunate that there are so many which are suitable for growing with the other choice alpines. Most are lime tolerant; they prefer a place in the sun but are happy in a well-drained soil. *Dianthus alpinus* is a gem, making a prostrate mat of foliage with flowers the size of half crowns on 3-inch (7-cm) stems. The best forms have petals coloured rose to crimson. I always grow plants from seed unless tempted by an exceptionally good plant offered for sale in flower. *D. deltoides*, (The Maiden Pink), is too large for the small rock garden or scree at 8 inches (20 cm) high. The colours range from scarlet through pink to pure white. Far more acceptable is our own native 'Cheddar Pink', *D. gratianopolitanus*, which forms mats of low grey foliage, and has the loveliest, most sweetly scented pink flowers imaginable. Never growing much above 6 inches (15 cm), it makes good ground cover with some of the thymes. *D. pavonius (neglectus)* grows wild in lime-free soil and stars the turf with pink flowers at Lautaret. The backs of the petals are always buff-coloured, a characteristic passed on to its offspring.

Draba trails a long tail of two hundred or more species. Many are not particularly interesting, others moderately so, while a few are really choice. *Draba aizoides*, a rare native in Britain, is common in European mountains. The hard, tight, bristly rosettes of leaves and yellow flowers on 2-inch (5-cm) stems are a worth-while addition to a wall or scree garden.

There are some plants which charm and delight without being stridently beautiful, and the Mountain Avens, *Dryas octopetala*, is certainly one of these. The small, dark green, oak-shaped leaves show off the large white, short-stemmed flowers with a central boss of yellow stamens to good effect. This is a very desirable shrublet, which, unless it is kept in gritty soil, grows too well and never flowers.

Had I to choose one plant which encapsulates all the attributes of beauty and character which are possessed in varying degrees by so many of the alpine plants, *Eritrichium nanum* would gain the award. My first encounter was on a visit to Mont Cenis. I had spent the whole day looking at the choicest flowers that this richly endowed area affords – *Viola cenisia, Campanula cenisia, Saxifraga retusa*, to name but a few. I decided to climb higher, and there it was, the eritrichium, a dense, silver-haired cushion of electric blue flowers with primrose-yellow centres. It is the complete, perfect, high-mountain plant, and is hopelessly difficult to cultivate even in an alpine house. The picture, like

Daphne cneorum

Right: *Eritrichium nanum*, the 'King of the Alps'

vivid blue bosses on a shield of stone, is still clearly memorable.

Gentians have given me pleasure from when, while still a schoolboy, I first became aware of plants as individuals. *Gentiana verna* grows quite near to the school I attended. The deep, azure-blue flowers on short stems open in April to May. In the garden a humus-rich soil is the best, and the roots should be kept well watered in dry weather. *G. acaulis* is a friendly plant and grows in any rich, well-drained soil. I once used several dozen plants as an edging to a bed of HT roses, and they flowered splendidly. The brilliant, dark blue, trumpet-shaped flowers rise on short stalks from the dark green leaf rosettes. Both gentians will grow from divisions or seed.

Geraniums are another of the indispensables. Certainly *Geranium cinereum subcaulescens* with crimson, black-eyed flowers on 6 to 8 inch (15 to 20 cm) stems, is a very comely rock plant. Though the wood crane's-bill *G. sylvaticum* is a little robust for the rock garden proper, the cup-shaped bluish-purple flowers look well in association with dwarf shrubs planted on the outskirts. Height is around 15 inches (38 cm).

Of *Leontopodium alpinum* much has been said and sung; certainly, it is a well-loved, though by no means lovely, alpine plant. Grey-green leaves and white felted flowers will furnish a corner in full sun given average soil. It is easily raised from seed.

Linaria alpina from the scree slopes in the European Alps is more annual than perennial with me, but it perpetuates itself by means of seed without becoming a weed. Blue-grey leaves decked with violet, orange-throated flowers are the gardener's reward for a place in full sun on a well-drained soil.

The 'Alpine poppy', *Papaver alpinum*, is one of the most difficult plants to photograph, as even a fragment of breeze sets the flowers waving. I have seen the plants grow on steep scree slopes: tufts of fern-like foliage topped by flowers of white, pink, or yellow. My choice would be the variety *P. a. kerneri* with large yellow, paper-textured blooms in early summer. A pinch of seed scattered on gritty soil is all the effort required from the cultivator.

Below left: *Geranium sylvaticum*
Below: *Gentiana acaulis*

Linaria alpina

Papaver alpinum

I found the little *Polygala chamaebuxus* growing in moist peat soil on the same north slope as *Daphne cneorum*. Like a miniature box shrub in foliage, it grows in the hollow wall and is rarely if ever without a crop of yellow- and cream-lipped flowers. The form 'Grandiflora', with red and yellow blossom, is equally desirable. Though in nature polygala grows in partial shade, the hollow wall in my garden has proved acceptable. A neat, compact shrublet 4 inches (10 cm) high, massed with flowers, this makes a very creditable addition to any collection of rock plants. Propagation is by rooted offshoots lifted in May.

There are some shrubs which I consider essential when planting a simulated alpine landscape, and *Potentilla fruticosa* is one. I choose the dwarf forms which grow out rather than up. Full sun is needed for the yellow- or white-flowered varieties, partial shade for those with red or orange petals. Almost any soil will suit them except an oozing swamp. 'Longacre' and 'Goldfinger' are excellently dwarf and free flowering with me.

Primulas and rhododendrons deserve, even command, a chapter to themselves, and are dealt with elsewhere in this book.

When is an anemone not an anemone? The answer seems to be, when the botanists decree it shall be pulsatilla. I still think of pulsatilla as anemone or 'Windflowers', though this is now incorrect. *Pulsatilla alpina* with white flowers and *P. a. apiifolia* with rich yellow flowers are frequenters of the alpine meadows. Both grow well in acid or alkaline soil, but at 18 or 24 inches (46 or 51 cm) high are too tall for the rock garden proper. Grow the

Saxifraga oppositifolia

plants from seed, and prick them off into pots, for they do hate root disturbance at any stage.

The sight vivid in memory of *P. alpina* in full bloom across a sloping hillside with snow-capped mountains behind, almost persuades me that this and not eritrichium is the 'King of the Alps'. The flowers, cupped in a filigree of fern-like foliage, are white with golden stamens, the outer sepals bewhiskered with silky gold and purple hairs. In seconds the colour changes from pink to gold to opal white – a delightful spring picture. I have never seen the same qualities reflected in cultivation, though *P. vernalis* is not hard to grow in humus-rich soil.

Ranunculus glacialis resists all attempts to wean it from mountain slope to garden. In nature the wide-spreading tufts of grey-green leaves, like those of an aconite, spread far and wide, often most luxuriantly in very wet but obviously free-draining soil beside mountain tarns. The very large, pure white, golden-centred flowers deepen with age to rose-red. Respect slowly replaces covetousness for this most determined mountaineer.

One of the largest families, Saxifraga, is also sufficiently diverse in character to warrant further division into sub-sections. Some grow in rock crevices on sheer cliff faces, others ribbon the stones with bands of scarlet along the mountain streams. The Kabschia section form tight mounds of attractively rounded rosettes of foliage. Brightly coloured, short-stemmed flowers appear in early spring. The hollow wall or very gritty scree is suitable, though pot culture in the alpine house is even better.

The Euaizoonia section contains all those species with silvered foliage. Long branching panicles of white flowers, spotted pink or red, are a feature in spring. I grow them in the crevices or between rocks of weathered limestone. Saxifraga

Saxifraga 'Valerie Finnis'

Sempervivum tectorum var. alpinum

Soldanella alpina

section Porphyrion includes two very easy-to-grow gems in *Saxifraga oppositifolia* and *S. retusa*. Both I found growing wild, either along the edge of glacial streams or the verges of mountain pools. *S. oppositifolia* makes a creeping mat of foliage starred with red-purple flowers in April to May. *S. retusa* is neater and more congested, with deeper red flowers. Both grow in lime-free scree with extra peat added, and a large stone alongside to keep the roots cool.

Sempervivums always give me the impression that they can live on fresh air and water. They grow quite luxuriantly on stone slate house roofs. There are fifty or so species and numerous hybrids, most of which are easy to grow in well-drained soil providing humus is added. Wall crevices, cracks between rocks, even the edge of a gravel path will suit. I remember seeing *Sempervivum tectorum var. alpinum* growing wild on a railway embankment in the Swiss Alps. *S. arachnoideum*, the 'Cobweb houseleek', is most decorative; the network of silver hairs over the rosettes of leaves are a characteristic, and in due season pink flowers add to the charm of this species.

In the high alpine scrubland, seeming to erupt through the melting snow, *Soldanella alpina* makes the most of early spring sunshine. Deep blue flowers, bell-shaped and fringed, nodding over rounded dark green leaves make the climb to discover them a small toll to pay. My search for *S. montana* was never rewarded, so instead I grow the plant in my garden. It is larger in all its parts than *S. alpina*; the deep blue, fringed bells sway to every breeze on 6-inch (15-cm) stems.

Alpine plants offer so many alluring fields of study that it is easy to become so engrossed in their cultivation that all other avenues of gardening are looked on as unworthy of attention.

2
Tulips

The story of the tulip is one of the brightest patterns woven into the historical tapestry of garden plants. Fortunately, the early history of the tulip is well documented, which is not surprising, and the text is fascinating to read.

As a species, tulips occur naturally in Europe, North Africa, and through to West and Central Asia, so the majority are hardy enough to be grown outdoors in the British Isles. The name Tulipa is derived from 'tuliban', a Persian or Turkish word meaning a turban. Though the splendidly colourful hybrid tulips dominate the garden scene, the species from which they have been developed are equally worthy of consideration. Their beauty, less garish, persuades rather than commands. The tulip appears to have been brought to this country some time in the last quarter of the sixteenth century. Certainly, there are records of tulip bulbs being grown in Antwerp in 1562, though they had been cultivated as a garden flower in Turkey probably from the beginning of the century. In the year 1554 an ambassador to the court of Suleiman the Magnificent saw tulips growing, almost certainly hybrids. Seeds were delivered to Vienna, and the first recorded illustration of the flower was made in 1561. This bloom, a cultivated hybrid which was first thought to be a species, *Tulipa gesneriana*, could be termed the progenitor of all modern tulips.

Carolus Clusius (Jules Charles de l'Ecluse), prefect of the Royal Medicinal Garden, Prague, received some of the first seeds, and, interestingly he was the one to mention the first double tulip. Clusius continued working with tulips following his appointment as Professor of Botany in Leiden. Who could have foreseen in the year 1600, while Clusius and, no doubt, other like-minded gardeners were raising bulbs from seed and observing the flowers, that in thirty years fortunes would be made, then lost again, over the sale of bulbs? The 1630s saw such an explosion of interest in the newest colour forms that bulbs changed hands for hundreds of pounds each. It is hard to imagine the tulip, familiar garden flower that it is, as an object of greedy speculation. Eventually 'Tulipomania', as it was called, reached a fever pitch until, in 1637, the bottom fell out of the market, halting further speculation in bulb trading. Thousands of people must have been ruined when the market collapsed; fortunately

Tulipa fosteriana 'Cantata'

the tulip survived to become one of Holland's major export industries. Only recently has the study of virus diseases revealed that the valued and much sought after striped and variously coloured blooms of the seventeenth century were not a product of the hybridiser's art; their characteristics were, and still are, caused by virus infection.

The glory and variety of colour which tulips possess, their versatility, offering species suitable for the rock garden, window box, and massed bedding schemes, have assured for them a secure place in the gardener's affection and esteem for almost four hundred years. During that time there have been further peaks of interest. In the 1850s catalogues listed over a thousand varieties, with several of the newest introductions priced at £100 each. There is a record of single bulbs being sold in Holland

during the same period for over £600. Fortunately, the present-day price per bulb enables the interested gardener to grow tulips without having to mortgage the house in order to pay for the indulgence. Modern nursery catalogues issue lists of varieties as extensive as those of the mid-nineteenth century, and in gardening terms the lists are divided into sections.

The group known as the 'Single Early' tulips offers a wide range of colours and is excellent for bedding work. They grow from 14 to 20 inches (35 to 50 cm), which is low enough to prevent them from being decapitated by boisterous spring winds. Because they flower early they are ready for lifting in good time, and the soil can be prepared for planting with summer bedding. Though it is not possible to mention more than a few varieties, of those I have grown 'Keizerskroon' with large red blooms edged with yellow, carried on 14-inch (35-cm) stems, has always proved satisfactory. Indeed, any garden plant would need to be possessed of special merit still to be listed three hundred years after being introduced, for 'Keizerskroon' is said to date from 1681. Another variety which I find most agreeable is 'Couleur Cardinal', which again grows only 14 inches (35 cm) high, with dark red blooms faintly tinged with purple on the outside; it is one of the most weather-resistant tulips I have tried.

For early flowering in pots, the lovely, golden-orange-petalled 'General de Wet' or the crisper yellow 'Bellona' will often be showing colour in February. 'Bellona' distils a pleasant fragrance, a quality not usually associated with tulips.

'Double Early' tulips express a quite different character. The multiplication of the petals is acknowledged in the descriptive popular name, 'Paeony-flowered tulip'. All the varieties I have

Above: *Tulipa* 'Bellona'

Top right: *Tulipa* 'Peach Blossom'
Below right: *Tulipa* 'Duc Van Tol'

grown are short stemmed, which makes them excellent material for use in patio tubs and window boxes. Two of the Double Early varieties proved useful for early colour in a cold greenhouse when grown in pots. Bulbs of the rich scarlet-flowered 'Carlton' and the equally impressive buttercup-yellow 'Hytuna' were potted up in peat-based compost in October. The pots were plunged outdoors until late December before being moved into the unheated greenhouse. Both varieties were in full bloom during March, and all their beauty could be enjoyed as they were not sullied by the weather. They can, of course, be planted outdoors in October or November to flower at the normal time in April. For those who enjoy a composed association I would recommend the pink blooms of 'Peach Blossom' mixed with the dark blue of *Scilla* 'Spring Beauty'.

Several crosses have been made between the original groups to produce varieties which flower at a time roughly between those of the two parents. 'Mendel' tulips arrived as a result of a cross between the very early-blooming 'Duc Van Tol' and several Darwin tulips. The combination resulted in new varieties like 'Van der Eerden', a bright crimson-red, which lends itself very well to pot cultivation indoors; and the strikingly tinted 'Orange Wonder' in shades of bronze, scarlet, and orange. Colour combinations of this degree need careful handling in the

Above: *Tulipa* 'Duc Van Tol Aurora'

Tulipa 'Peerless Pink'

Top: *Tulipa* 'Pink Supreme'
Above: *Tulipa* 'Carnova'

garden design, with the cool blue of forget-me-not or muscari to act as a soothing undertone.

The Triumph tulips were the product of a pollen exchange between the Darwin group and the more vigorous-growing Single Early tulips. Hybrid vigour possibly explains the strong sturdy stems and longer-lasting flowers which make Triumph varieties such good cut flowers. Of those I have tried 'Preludium' is well worth a place, the petals deep rose fading gradually to pure white at the base. 'Reforma', sulphur-yellow, and 'Peerless Pink' flushed with mauve, are also sturdy and long lasting in bloom. *T.* 'Marco Polo' is a newer variety with a crimson colour flushed with yellow.

Tall-growing tulips are breath-takingly beautiful when massed in beds, and are featured in parks department displays throughout the British Isles. Darwin tulips 'Bleu Aimable', lavender-mauve, 'Pink Supreme', deep pink, and the unusual 'Carnova' are impressive. Darwin hybrids such as these are produced by crossing the brilliant scarlet-flowered species *T. fosteriana* with the vigorous Darwins to produce tall plants with large flowers so vividly coloured that the very air around the area of the garden in which they are growing seems warmed by the display. 'Holland's Glorie', with large, orange-red blooms grows 24 inches (61 cm) high, and 'Red Matador' is so aggressively scarlet that only against the dark background of a conifer hedge can its quality be fully appreciated. As material for floral decoration, the regal magnificence of the tulip 'Queen Wil-helmina' is quite superb. Tall at nearly 30 inches (76 cm), the petals, orange-scarlet paling at the edges, are in fact too large in the isolation of a bedding display, but most effective planted in groups down a shrub or herbaceous border.

For some years I grew a mixture of the Rembrandt varieties in a bed which included a fine specimen of the grey-leaved weeping pear, *Pyrus salicifolia* 'Pendula'. I never did adjust to the Joseph's-coat pattern produced by the multi-coloured, flaked, striped, and feathered petals. Named varieties enable the colour scheme to be adjusted and modulated to a level I find more acceptable. In practice, Rembrandts excite the interest of flower arrangers more than the enthusiasm of gardeners.

Cottage or May-flowering tulips are very hard to categorise. In catalogues it is not unusual to find a variety listed under Darwin in one grower's list, and under Cottage in another. So far as I can discover, in the early part of the nineteenth century a group of enthusiasts collected together the late-flowering tulips from established colonies existing in the gardens of that period, and used the best as breeding stock. They are strong growing, with rounded flowers carried on stems up to 30 inches (76 cm) high. 'Golden Harvest', a deep lemon, is earlier-flowering than most of the others, and is usually in colour by late April. 'Greenland', with green-tinged petals edged with pink, is a popular variety for use in floral arrangements. 'Sweet Harmony' is also useful for cutting; the lemon-yellow flowers with a white margin stand for a long time in floral arrangements. A newer variety, 'Burgundy Lace', is an attractive scarlet-red.

Though the Lily-flowered varieties bloom at the same time as, and are often grouped with, Cottage tulips, in flower shape

Tulipa 'Greenland'

Above: *Tulipa* 'Maytime'
Right: *Tulipa* 'Mariette'

they are quite distinct. Long, narrow-waisted blooms with reflexing petals present a graceful appearance in contrast to the ovoid flowers of other May-flowering varieties. Usually they are shorter in stature, the stem length ranging between 15 and 24 inches (38 and 61 cm). 'Mariette', with deep pink, emphatically recurved petals, grows up to 20 inches (51 cm) high. 'Maytime', lilac with a white edge, and 'West Point', yellow, are shorter and look well when grouped together.

'Elizabeth Arden' is a variety of the Darwin hybrid type which I first planted twenty-six years ago. The petals are coloured rose-violet on the outside with a salmon-rose interior – an improbable combination which proves most effective.

For me Parrot tulips are an acquired taste, the clusters of twisted and fringed petals, often measuring 10 inches (25 cm) across, look more like the flowers of the paeony. A massed planting in full bloom on a warm May day is spectacular. 'Orange Favourite', 'Faraday', 'Texas Flame', 'Flaming Parrot', and 'Black Parrot' would serve as an introductory planting.

The bulbs to be grown outdoors are best planted in late October or November – a most inhospitable time of year, it would seem, but earlier planting means that the bulbs are too soon into growth, which exposes the foliage and flower buds to frost. On heavy soils 4 inches (10 cm) will be sufficiently deep to bury the bulbs; lighter soils encourage deeper planting, to 6 or 8 inches (15 or 20 cm) below the surface. The distance apart varies according to whether the bulbs are used in a formal bedding

Top left: *Tulipa* 'Texas Flame'
Below left: *Tulipa* 'Orange Favourite'
Right: *Tulipa* 'Flaming Parrot'

scheme or to achieve a random effect. For formal work 4 to 6 inches (10 to 15 cm) apart according to variety is adequate.

Any good garden soil which is well drained and has not been freshly manured will grow tulips well. Where the soil condition needs improving, work in a dressing of well-rotted compost or moist peat after lifting out summer bedding plants in late September. As tulips thrive best in an alkaline soil, provision should be made for this if the soil is at all acid in reaction by dressing the surface with chalk or ground limestone either before or, as I have often done, after planting, particularly if the soil is on the heavy side of medium texture.

Though the tulip species and the hybrids produced from them are less assertive than the Darwin, Triumph, and other bedding varieties, they are, particularly for the owners of small gardens, of equal value. They are beautiful in flower, adaptable in cultivation indoors or for planting outdoors in the rock garden, borders, patios, or window boxes. There are some – *Tulipa tarda* is an example in my own garden – which have spread into quite sizeable colonies over the years. Bulbs planted in a well-drained soil will add another colour dimension to the garden scene in spring. I leave some of the species in the ground all the year round, maintaining the vigour of the bulbs by regular feeding with bone meal and compost top dressing.

Unless seed is needed for raising new stock I take off the flower heads as petals fall. The leaves are not cleared away until they wither and part easily from the bulbs.

One of the most popular species is the water-lily tulip, *T. kaufmanniana*, which combines a very compact habit with large, brilliantly coloured flowers. Indeed, so many hybrids have been introduced from crosses between this species with *T. fosteriana* and the ever-productive *T. greigii*, that the choice is so wide as to be bewildering. In the type species, *T. kaufmanniana* grows only about 6 inches (15 cm) high. The creamy-yellow flower is tinged pink on the outside and rises out of a basal rosette of grey-green

Below: *Tulipa tarda*

leaves very early in spring. Of the varieties I have grown 'Shakespeare', the flowers a mixture of salmon, apricot, and orange on 5-inch (13-cm) high stems, are reliable and pleasantly unusual. 'Stresa', yellow flushed with red, and 'Heart's Delight' a pinky white flushed with red, will bring colour to any garden on a cold spring day.

In spite of several attempts I cannot be certain that the bulbs purchased as *T. fosteriana* were the true species. Though the flower colour, scarlet with a yellow-edged basal blotch, is faithfully produced in each case, the height varies from a modest 7 inches (18 cm) in one group to an extreme 18 inches (46 cm) in another. Flower size shows a similar wide variation. Of the hybrids I would choose 'Princeps', vivid red blooms on 8-inch

Tulipa kaufmanniana 'Heart's Delight'

Below left: *Tulipa kaufmanniana* 'Shakespeare'
Below: *Tulipa kaufmanniana* 'Stresa'

Tulipa fosteriana 'Cantata'

(20-cm) stems, or 'Cantata', whose bright scarlet petals are narrowly reflexed and beautifully shaped.

T. greigii has such attractively marked leaves that it would almost be worth including as a foliage plant. The species and all the varieties I have grown derived from it have leaves which are veined with maroon or purple-brown. Brilliantly coloured flowers open on short stems during April and early May. Though they are dwarf enough to be accommodated in the rock garden, I prefer to use these vivid flowers in massed bedding, tubs, or window boxes. Given free choice of all the varieties on offer, I would select 'Red Riding Hood' with scarlet-red petals, which I grow alongside an elaeagnus with golden leaves to achieve an effect which verges on the violent. The variety 'Dreamboat' has a

Tulipa greigii 'Red Riding Hood'

Tulipa pulchella 'Humilis'

delightful colour combination, each petal with an amber-yellow ground colour shaded with red.

The species tulips offer such a wealth of beauty and interest that it is hard to resist becoming a collector. There are some which, like the tiny *T. pulchella*, will succeed only in northern gardens when grown in pots. Violet-red flowers on 4- to 6-inch (10- to 15-cm) stems nestle close amongst the leaves in March. Others are more robust, sensibly flowering when there is promise if not an actuality of spring, and so can be safely planted outdoors. *T. clusiana* (lady tulip) grows 12 inches (30 cm) high, and is white with the three outer petals carrying a bold cherry-red stripe. I grow this tulip in company with forget-me-nots and a dark-green-foliaged dwarf conifer, so that the flowers are shown in bold contrast. *T. batalinii* looks so primly modest that I like to see it in association with cottage garden flowers – pinks, pansy, and the smoky-grey foliage of 'Lad's love'. Both the type species *T. batalinii* and the hybrid 'Bronze Charm' are very compact-growing, being only 4 to 6 inches (10 to 15 cm) high. The former has lovely soft-yellow flowers; the hybrid has blossoms which vary between bronze and apricot. Mention must be made here of our own native tulip, *T. sylvestris*, still to be found growing wild in isolated pockets of the British Isles, and in cultivation at the Cambridge Botanic Gardens.

Tulipa sylvestris

Tulipa praestans 'Fusilier'

T. praestans is unusual in that instead of one flower, several orange-scarlet blooms are carried on a 12-inch (30-cm) stem. Both the species and hybrids – of which 'Fusilier' would be my choice – are good value as they do not need to be lifted each year. One group that I have planted among dwarf shrubs in the rock garden has flowered very creditably for the last four years.

The most perennial species I have grown is a native of Russia, *T. tarda*, illustrated on the cover of this book. This is so well suited by soil and climate that it has spread self-sown seedlings into a bed of crocus nearby. The leaf rosettes lie flat to support clusters of flowers which are white with a central yellow eye. Growing to about 5 inches (13 cm) high, they can be comfortably accommodated on the outskirts of the rock garden.

Similar in character to *T. tarda*, the Iranian species *T. urumiensis* with star-shaped yellow flowers has also proved suitable in an alpine context. The petals are yellow-stained bronze, opening to show deeper yellow anthers. *T. biflora* is another attractive species. A native of Russia, it has pale green leaves, and each stem bears three to five white flowers with a yellow eye in early spring. Not spectacular, just quietly and obligingly pleasant.

Species tulips in no way compete with the large-flowered garden hybrids. There is a place for both even in the smaller garden context. The large-flowered garden hybrids are best lifted when the foliage has withered. After being dried off they can then be cleaned of soil or other debris before being stored until required for replanting in autumn. I leave species tulips in the ground without disturbance; colonies which die out under this treatment can be replaced at reasonable cost.

Tulipa batalinii 'Bronze Charm'

3
Rhododendrons

Rhododendrons present a bewildering array to the novice gardener as he scans the list of species and varieties available. There are somewhere between seven hundred and a thousand species, showing such a marked difference in character that at times it is hard to accept that they belong to the same genus. To compare a tiny, mat-forming midget only an inch or two (2·5 or 5 cm) high with a forest tree towering 40 feet (12 m) above one's head requires a mental dexterity that only a specialist can acquire. Fortunately, the amateur need not become embroiled in the finer chemical or botanical details that separate one species from another. Though it is nice to know that the genus *Rhodod-endron* subdivides into groups and series, it is information essential only to the botanist or specialist grower.

The rhododendron story is fascinating, beginning with the plant explorers who at considerable personal risk collected plants or seed in China, Tibet, India, Burma, and Nepal. Their names are firmly established in garden history: Sir Joseph Hooker, Robert Fortune, George Forrest, and the French missionaries Abbé Delavay and Père David. There is no epitaph more worthy or enduring than the species named after them.

There is one limitation which prevents all who would from growing rhododendrons. A lime-free soil is essential. Some rhododendrons can be persuaded by generous mulches of peat and frequent applications of trace elements to grow in an alkaline soil, but they never really thrive. Given an acid soil, plenty of moisture, and shelter from cold winds, they are unsurpassed in beauty of flower, or infinite variety of form and foliage. Shelter from cold wind is a prime requirement for all Asiatic rhododen-drons except the small-leafed species (*Lepidote*) which clothe the mountains above the highest level of tree growth – between 10 000 and 15 000 feet (3 000 and 4 600 m).

Experience has shown that the majority of species rhododen-drons are quite well able to stand the severest winter likely to be inflicted on the British Isles, providing the cold is unbroken. Indeed, under natural conditions they are dormant because of the severe weather for six or seven months of the year. Condi-tions in the average winter here are very different, with long periods of mild weather which cause flower buds to put down

A delightful woodland setting
for rhododendrons at Exbury
Gardens, near Southampton

their protecting scales and start to open prematurely, only to be
killed by a sudden bleak frost. Alternate freeze and thaw can
continue even into May, killing the current year's blooms and
blackening the young growth, which also destroys prospects for
the following season.

The ideal site on which to grow rhododendrons would be in
open glades in woodland, consisting of deep-rooted trees like
oak. Other trees are suitable only if they do not compete for
moisture and food with the shallow, surface-rooting rhododendron. The smaller-leafed species are better suited in a more open
position, associating well with low-growing heathers and dwarf
conifers. I prepare the soil in advance of planting by working in
heavy dressings of moist peat, leaf mould, or well-rotted manure.
This results in the moist, almost spongy root run in which all
ericaceous plants revel. When planting, it is important to make
certain that the top of the root ball is level with the soil surface.

To ensure against its drying out, finish off with a 2-inch (5-cm) covering of peat or leaf mould. Deep planting can kill even healthy rhododendrons; the high planting and peat mulch are the best safeguards. The best time to plant is in April to May when growth is active during periods of warm, moist weather. I have moved plants in full bloom, kept them well-watered afterwards without their losing a single leaf.

The first species to be introduced and recorded were *R. hirsutum* and *R. ferrugineum* from the European Alps. *R. hirsutum* arrived first – a small shrub with clusters of tubular flowers opening in June. Certainly, John Tradescant was growing this species in his garden in the mid-seventeenth century. Not until nearly a hundred years later is there any mention of *R. ferrugineum* being in cultivation. Popularly known as the Alpine rose, the flowers are tubular, rose-crimson, opening in tight trusses during June.

In 1736 the first of several species arrived from America, to be closely followed in 1763 by what most people regard as the archetypal rhododendron, the ubiquitous *R. ponticum* from Armenia and Asia Minor. Now it is so well naturalised as to be a weed nuisance in forestry plantations. It is useful as an informal hedge and will make, in time, a large shrub 15 feet (4·6 m) high. The flower colour varies from lilac-pink to mauve. In the past it has often been used as a root-stock on which to graft scions of named varieties. Occasionally the scion dies, and the root-stock survives to establish yet another colony of common *ponticum*.

Early in the nineteenth century two species were discovered. *R. caucasicum*, from the mountain of that name in the Caucasus, was found growing virtually on the snow line. Six years later the second species, *R. catawbiense*, was introduced from the Allegheny mountains in the United States of America. The material was at hand for the plant breeder to work with, and the result was several notable hardy hybrids. The best-known is the early-flowering 'Christmas Cheer', densely compact in growth with pink blossoms fading to white.

Rhododendron ponticum

Rhododendron arboreum

Not until the advent of *R. arboreum* in the early nineteenth century did it become possible to produce the scarlet and vivid crimson varieties which are such an illuminating feature of our woodlands and gardens. *R. arboreum* was the first Himalayan species to be introduced. The blood-red flowers open during the coldest months of the year in favoured localities, the first colour shows in January, so the display is frequently ruined by frost. I have seen specimens 30 feet (9 m) high laden down with globular heads of red-petalled flowers glowing in March sunshine, making the whole tree a vibrant cone of colour.

Fascinating though the natural species are, it is the hybrids which have ensured the rhododendron's continuing popularity as a garden rather than a park or woodland shrub. The crossing of the red *R. arboreum* on to the old *R. catawbiense* and *R. ponticum* hybrids really heralded the birth of the vast range of garden hybrid rhododendrons available today. All this was only a first tentative step, for it merely pre-empted the mass introduc-

Rhododendron falconeri

tion of new species from the Himalayas, which began with Sir Joseph Hooker's expedition in 1848. Like anyone else who grows rhododendrons for any length of time, I have my favourites, and it is surprising how many are contained in the forty-three species collected by Hooker during the two years of the expedition – species of such quality that they alone would have raised the status of the genus as garden plants to share pride of place with the rose.

The large-leafed *R. falconeri*, with huge trusses of creamy-white flowers each printed with a stain of purple on the throat, must have taken the gardening world by storm when it bloomed for the first time. Like all the large-leafed species, it needs the shelter provided by a woodland glade. Another of the Hooker introductions, *R. ciliatum*, which grows wild on steep mountain slopes if the soil is moist enough, or along the margins of streams,

Rhododendron thomsonii

at up to 12 000 feet (3 600 m) in the Sino-Himalayas, is a complete contrast to *R. falconeri*. This species grows to only 3 or 4 feet (0·9 or 1·2 m) high with 3-inch-long (8-cm) leaves fringed with hair, and bell-shaped flowers of a delicate shell-pink. The buds start to break early, and year after year the flowers on my plants were blackened by frost. Eventually, in a kill-or-cure treatment I moved the plants out into an open north-facing border. Here growth is compact, and most years the flowers open late enough to escape the frost.

R. thomsonii with scarlet petals so textured that they present a waxed appearance, and lovely glaucous grey-blue foliage is, undoubtedly, pleasing though requiring woodland conditions to achieve full potential. Indeed, the list reads like *Who's Who*; with the yellow *R. campylocarpum* and the superb but tender *R. griffithianum* to tempt the appetite it is not surprising that in what now seems to be excessive zeal gardeners rushed to plant them. Ignorance of the ultimate height or spread of the species being planted should impose restraint, or within a very short time – as happened in so many newly created rhododendron gardens – the plants become overcrowded so that all the beauty of form is lost. Though *R. griffithianum* is not amongst the hardiest species, this did not prevent it being used to cross-pollinate other species. Indeed, a hybrid of *R. griffithianum* crossed with a hybrid of that patriarchal *R. arboreum* produced one of the most admired hybrids ever, the iron-constitutioned 'Pink Pearl'. *R. ciliatum* is also parent to a noteworthy hybrid in the early-flowering *R. × praecox*, whose rose-purple flowers open in March, adding a contrast to the predominantly yellow theme of that season.

Of all the plant hunters, George Forrest is the one to whom gardeners owe the greatest debt. The total number of plants he collected amounted to over thirty thousand: a prodigious achievement when related to the difficult terrain he was working in, the primitive conditions he had to live under, and the archaic transport available, both for himself and the dispatch of the plants from China to this country. The list of rhododendrons Forrest discovered in the Tali mountains of north-west Yunnan reveals the extent of his contribution to our knowledge of the genus. Particularly valuable were the many alpine dwarf species of rhododendrons which he imported. Like all plants of modest stature they exercise a peculiar fascination. In practical terms, twenty dwarf species or hybrids can be accommodated in the area occupied by one mature, taller-growing species which frequently covers an area 150 feet (46 m) in circumference. The dwarf species will grow in open situations, making themselves at home in rock or heather garden in conditions which would desiccate the large-leafed rhododendrons. *R. forrestii*, the species which bears his name, forms a mat of foliage only an inch or two (2·5 to 5 cm) high. The large, bell-shaped flowers borne in pairs are bright scarlet. Even in moist soil and shade, which it prefers, my plant rarely flowers. In this event a hybrid between *R. forrestii repens* and the tender but eminently desirable *R. griersonianum* is to be preferred. This hybrid, called 'Elizabeth', is of dwarf habit; the clustered heads of rich-red flowers open in April.

Rhododendron augustinii in the
Royal Botanic Garden, Edinburgh

Forrest, amongst others, also imported the dwarf yellow-flowered, aromatic-leafed *R. sargentianum*. This forms a lovely contrast to the even more compact, deep purple-rose blossoms of a species he introduced in 1910 called, very aptly, '*R. prostratum*'. So then the number of species grew in quantity and in variety of foliage and flower, surely enough to fill every possible situation or need which our gardens afford.

What, in fact, did happen was that anyone and everyone who grew rhododendrons began to cross-pollinate, so that new hybrids were manufactured in such numbers that muddle and confusion were inevitable. To make any sort of gardening sense, hybridisation must be embarked upon with a specific purpose in mind. To do this parents are carefully selected for qualities of leaf, flower, hardiness, or habit of growth. One is designated as the female or seed parent. When the flowers are still immature they are enclosed in a muslin bag to exclude completely insects which could cross-fertilise the flower prematurely. When the petals expand, the stamens (or male organs) are removed with a pair of nail tweezers, which prevents self-pollination of the flower. When the stigma becomes sticky – a sure sign of maturity for pollination – anthers from the chosen male parent which are shedding pollen are rubbed over the stigma of the female. The muslin bag is kept in place until it is obvious that the cross has taken. I always make a note of the exact parentage – male and female – and the date the cross was made. Hybrids are not acceptable without a birth certificate, so to speak. The seed capsules take anything up to ten months before the case starts to open at the tip, indicating that the seeds are ready for dispersal. I harvest the capsules, then leave them on saucers or newspapers until the seeds drop out.

For sowing, a half pot 4 or 5 inches (10 or 13 cm) in diameter will do very well. The compost I have found suitable is 2 parts sieved peat, 1 part sharp lime-free sand. Fill the pot with the mixture to within half an inch (1·2 cm) of the rim. A piece of zinc or broken pot over the drainage hole is advisable, though not essential. Firm the compost lightly with a pot press, then sow the seed thinly over the surface. Keep well-watered by plunging the pot up to the rim in rain-water – unlike tap-water this is sure to be lime-free. I protect the pots with butter muslin at all stages, before and after germination, to prevent scorching of the leaves. The seedlings are grown on for a year, or even two years, before being pricked off into an ericaceous compost for growing on.

Making a choice from the thousands of different species and varieties available is not easy, even with thirty years' experience. The following are good garden value, starting first with the species – though it must be admitted that they lack the adaptability of the hybrids. *R. augustinii* is a tall-growing shrub with small leaves; the best forms have deep blue flowers which open in late April to May. It is a good, quick-growing species which looks particularly pleasing in patterned shade. It is easily propagated by means of cuttings made from young growths. These are taken in July into a rooting compost of 2 parts lime-free sand and 1 part peat. *R. orbiculare* is a dense evergreen shrub

Top left: *Rhododendron orbiculare*
Below left: *Rhododendron wardii*

with clusters of pink flowers borne in April to May. *R. wardii* is one of the most outstanding yellow-flowered species to be introduced from China. It is sufficiently attractive to warrant a sheltered corner of a large garden. *R. vernicosum* is one of George Forrest's introductions still to be found growing in the Royal Botanic Garden, Edinburgh. The young buds are pink, and the white flowers are at their best in early May. *R. cinnabarinum* is a medium-sized shrub in all the forms available; a most beautiful and desirable decoration for the garden. The flowers are pendant tubes of bright cinnabar-red. An added charm is revealed in the blue-green of the young unfolding leaves. *R. haematodes* ranks amongst the pick of Chinese rhododendrons, with its neat, compact growth and dark green leaves, which are covered on the undersides with fox-red, felt-like hairs called indumentum. This character, exhibited by certain species, gives them a perennial beauty. In May to June *R. haematodes* displays scarlet-crimson, bell-shaped flowers. It is certainly, one of George Forrest's most praiseworthy introductions. In my last garden a bush had grown only 30 inches (76 cm) high by 36 inches (91 cm) across in twenty years. *R. impeditum*, one of the dwarf alpine shrublets at most 1 foot (30 cm) high, is a gem of the genus. Silvered foliage sets off the dark blue flowers. *R. pemakoense* is another very handsome dwarf alpine shrub. Of the two forms I have grown one spread by suckers. This is a very free-flowering little species; in April the 1-foot-high (30-cm) dome of leaves disappears under a screen of lilac-pink blooms. *R. prostratum* creeps along close to the ground, and is splendid for furnishing the north face of the rock garden. The flowers, which open almost flat, are crimson with darker spots.

Right: *Rhododendron cinnabarinum*

Above:
Rhododendron spinuliferum
Above right:
Rhododendron williamsianum
Right:
Rhododendron sinogrande

Below:
Rhododendron 'Curlew'
Below right:
Rhododendron fastigiatum

Rhododendron yakushimanum

An unnamed rhododendron seedling

There are several forms of the variable species *R. racemosum*. The best is the one originally collected by George Forrest known as 'Forrest's Dwarf'. The rufous-red branchlets wreathed in bright pink flowers are fit adornment for the most choice rock or shrub garden. *R. russatum* has received enough awards, including that of 'Garden Merit' from the Royal Horticultural Society in 1938, to warrant inclusion for the first-rate garden plant that it is. It grows about 3 feet (0·9 m) high; the foliage has a copper tint in early spring; and the flowers are deep violet with white shading in the throat. *R. williamsianum* has rounded leaves, bronze young growth, and beautifully formed pink, bell-shaped flowers. A sheltered position is advisable, as the buds show colour early and are liable to be frosted.

There are many more species. The magnificent-leafed *R. sinogrande, basilicum* and others of similar character are specialist plants, achieving their full beauty in the moister, warmer gardens of the west coast. An unusual looking species is *R. spinuliferum* which was flowering well in May at Wakehurst Gardens in Sussex. However, had I to choose just one species from the list, it would be, undoubtedly, *R. yakushimanum*. Found growing only on the mountain slopes of Yakushima Island, Japan, this really is a choice shrub for small or large garden. Over several years it will grow into a dome-shaped bush just 3 to 4 feet (0·9 to 1·2 m) high. Mature leaves are dark, glossy green above and brown-felted below. Young growths are silvered-grey suede in texture. Apple-blossom pink in bud, the flowers open in May and fade to white with age.

Dwarf rhododendrons are very popular in small gardens where space is at a premium. A favourite of mine is *R. fastigiatum* which grows to a height of 3 feet (0·9 m) and has a spread of 2 feet (60 m). The light-purple flowers open in April, and it makes an excellent grouping with heathers. Amongst the dwarf hybrids *R.* 'Pink Drift' flowers profusely in early May, whilst *R.* 'Curlew' is not only a compact plant ideal for the rock garden, but is often used as a parent for new varieties. More and more new varieties are arriving to join old established ones. Even as yet unnamed

Rhododendron luteum

seedlings seem to have that special quality which make the rhododendrons such popular garden shrubs.

Azaleas are very much a part of the family, so closely akin that they are now listed as rhododendrons. They require the same cultivation, though the majority of deciduous varieties will flower well in full sun so long as the soil is moist. One fully-hardy hybrid is *R.* 'Palestrina'. This has white flowers with a trace of green, and is a mass of bloom at Exbury Gardens in early May. There is a certain doubt about the hardiness of *R. schlippenbachii* which my experience denies – it is a very desirable garden plant. The rose pink, saucer-shaped flowers open on naked branches, to be followed by foliage which is purple-tinged when young. In the autumn the leaves turn crimson and gold before being shed.

The most popular of this group is the 'Honeysuckle azalea', *R. luteum* – my choice if I were allowed only one species to grow with *R. yakushimanum*. The primrose-yellow, fragrant flowers are a feature in May; then in October the leaves turn vivid shades of orange, red, and purple. Brilliant autumn colour is a feature of many deciduous azaleas.

All the species rhododendrons can be raised from seed sown in suitable lime-free compost – either the 2 parts peat, 1 part sand previously described, or the ericaceous mixture on sale in the

Azaleas in all their glory
at Exbury Gardens

garden shops. Seed saved from open-pollinated species may have been crossed with a different species or hybrid, so will not grow into an exact replica of the parent.

Small-leafed rhododendron, including the azaleas, will grow from cuttings made of semi-ripe young growth taken in July to August. All rhododendrons can be layered by means of branches which grow low enough to be pegged down into a mixture of peat and sand. Make a cut on the underside of the branch, halfway through and about 2 to 3 inches (5 to 8 cm) long. I pop a piece of sphagnum moss or peat into the cut so that it is held open, treat the wound with rooting powder, then peg the branch down firmly so that it is buried about 3 inches (8 cm) deep in the compost. I also place a heavy stone on top to make sure that it is held firm. Keep the layer well-watered in dry weather, and in eighteen months it should be rooted. Sever the layer from the parent bush two or three months before lifting it for transplanting elsewhere in the garden.

There are so many hybrids to choose from that the only way to get the right plant is to go along to a nursery when the bushes are in bloom. Check the flower colour and leaf shape, and if possible enquire what the ultimate height will be, then buy the one which fills all requirements.

4
Primulas

Primulas are distributed throughout the world. They extend in a band across North America, Europe, including the British Isles, northern India and Asia with the greatest concentration in the latter continent. Some of them, including the well-loved primrose, *Primula vulgaris*, are native to this country. Other natives are *P. veris*, *P. scotica* and *P. farinosa*. There are so many species – well over five hundred – occurring in such widely diverse habitats that Primulas offer a study in themselves. Some grow naturally in moist rock crevices high up in the mountains, whereas others colonise shady forest glades, open meadows, or ribbon the banks of streams with colour. A small percentage of primula species will grow quite happily under ordinary garden conditions. Others need special soils, or the shelter of a frame, or even a heated greenhouse. Such a wide diversity of cultural requirements offers interest to everyone from the novice to the most dedicated of gardeners. Each success acts as a spur to further effort.

There are members of the clan which have been much-loved garden plants for centuries and in consequence have a well-documented history. Our own native primrose, which grows in careless profusion in hedgerows, copses, and woodland from Scotland to the Mediterranean, is particularly well recorded.

Below left: *Primula vulgaris*
Below: *Primula vulgaris* (Double form)

Primula 'Penlan Strain'

Though the type species, the lovely *P. vulgaris*, is by no means easy to establish in the garden, the special garden forms developed from it show no such reluctance. To most people a primrose has yellow flowers, but coloured forms do occur in the wild. *P. vulgaris sibthorpii*, the 'Caucasian primrose', differs in the colour of the petals, which may be purple, red, lilac, white, or, rarely, yellow. The possibility of natural and induced variation is immediately obvious, and gardeners of three hundred years ago were quick to take advantage of this in practical terms. Until quite recently the production and maintenance of double-flowered forms were thought to depend on the plants being frequently lifted, clipped over, and transplanted, so it is surprising that any primrose survived – or gardeners, either. The first variation mentioned is a double cream-coloured flower with a sweet scent, for red or purple variations seem not to have occurred until the Caucasian primrose was distributed in the early 1600s. This blooms earlier than our native primrose, so cross-pollination would need to be contrived, although manipulation would hardly seem necessary as the Caucasian primrose is variable enough without hybridisation. By the mid-seventeenth century in one botanic garden there were growing blue, purple, and white single-flowered forms, but still only the one double-flowered variety. By the eighteenth century double varieties were established, including a double red. Then as now, if reports I have read are accurate, the double white is the easiest to grow, while the best forms of double red are the hardiest, at least in my experience. The source of many double primroses, Ireland, gives a clue to their cultivation in gardens: a sheltered, moist corner suits my plants very well. Varieties generally available are the splendid, four-hundred-year-old 'Double White'; 'Our Pat', amethyst-purple; 'Marie Crousse', violet-red; and 'Bon Accord Gem', rose-coloured. The variety I grew as 'G. F. Wilson' must, I think, be 'Quaker's Bonnet', and extremely difficult, in my experience, to keep alive. Every other year the plants need lifting and dividing, and are then replanted in a new site which has been prepared in advance by digging in, preferably, rotted cow manure, although peat, leaf mould or compost will do.

Primula 'Marie Crousse'

The 'polyanthus', *Primula × variabilis*, is the result of a union between the cowslip, *Primula veris*, and the primrose. Neither of the two parents is easy to establish in gardens, and yet the polyanthus product of the union is one of our most adaptable, tractable, and popular plants – and one of the mysteries of gardening, one of the many mysteries, for this is what captures then holds our interest. Crosses do occur in the wild, and the resulting seedlings are exactly like the oxlip. Indeed, I have found primroses, cowslips, and oxlips all growing together. I have also found cowslips growing alone, or primroses growing alone, but never the oxlip, even though it is considered a distinct species, *P. elatior*. The name 'polyanthus' occurs in seventeenth-century gardening journals, and by the end of the eighteenth century it had become a sought-after florist's flower. These very specialist varieties were, I suspect, the gold- and silver-laced varieties which today have almost disappeared from general commercial cultivation. Now, there are many strains of polyanthus in a wide selection of colours with individual blooms so large that some of the charm and character is being lost. However, many of the old and interesting colour forms still exist and are popular. Names like 'Jack in the Green', 'Jackanapes', and 'Hose in Hose' seem to add to the charm of the plant, and the 'Barnhaven' varieties remain ever popular.

A soil well-supplied with rotted manure or similar humus-forming material will suit polyanthus. The plants should be lifted and divided every second year, or they deteriorate even in the most suitable soil conditions. Alternatively, new stock can be raised from seed each year, for this ensures that you obtain well-flowered plants.

Above left: *Primula elatior*
Above: *Primula veris*

Above: *Primula* 'Hose in Hose'
Above right: *Primula* 'Barnhaven Gold'

The wild species of primula that we call *P. auricula*, of which 'Dusty Miller', is a garden cultivar, is in nature an alpine plant, and this gives a clue to the place which will best suit the species in the garden. They will tolerate a variety of soils if the drainage is good. I dig in a good supply of rotted compost, plus enough crushed stone to provide perfect drainage. As so often happens, hybrids have largely supplanted the species, and the cross between *P. auricula* and *P. hirsuta* was the first recorded,

Primula 'Barnhaven Blues'

resulting in a race of garden auricula collectively known as *P. pubescens*. These are smooth-leaved, and differ quite markedly from the specialist 'Show' and mealy-leaved 'Border' varieties which figure in the Primula Society shows. During the years 1650–1760 it almost became a cult flower, with the highly prized striped and edged show or florist varieties bringing sums in excess of £20 each. The white powder, farina, which dusts the leaves, is soon damaged if the plants are exposed to rain, as is the 'paste' on the centre of the flowers, so this section is cultivated as pot plants, and very handsome they are.

Some of the composts recommended for the proper cultivation of show auricula must have tested the devotion of even the enthusiasts: pigeon or goose dung, blood and similarly noxious materials are offered as essentials.

During the latter half of the nineteenth century came the Asiatic primula, from Sikkim, Nepal, the China–Tibet border – what an Aladdin's cave of plants this area is! Many of the new introductions proved hardier and easier to cultivate than the European species, so were welcomed with greater enthusiasm. The first of these, and still the most popular, is the 'Drumstick Primula', *P. denticulata*, discovered during the 1830s in upper Nepal. Any soil will suit this accommodating plant so long as it is never allowed to dry out. To make certain of the cool, moist root run in which this species delights I dig in compost, peat or well-rotted manure, and my plants flower excellently. Several good

Top: *Primula denticulata* 'Alba'
Above: *Primula denticulata*

colour forms have been selected, ranging from the cool lilac of the species, through to violet, pink, red and pure white. These are best increased by division, but seed is freely supplied and is easy to germinate. Height is 12 to 20 inches (30 to 51 cm) at flowering.

Another Himalayan species worthy of mention is *P. rosea*. A compact little plant, its rose-pink flowers are held 4 inches (10 cm) high, and are a delight in my garden in late April.

Before embarking on a survey of the most garden-worthy Asiatic primula, mention should be made of *P. farinosa* – our native 'Bird's-eye primrose' – which is easily grown in moist, peaty soil. The petal colour varies from light purple to lilac, pink, and a most delicate albino. The flower stems grow 10 inches (25 cm) high with a few or many flowers to a compact head. Seed will germinate two or three weeks after sowing, or old plants which readily form separate crowns may be divided after flowering. The other primula native to these islands is *P. scotica*; found only in the most northerly parts of Scotland, it grows in damp pasture land.

More important from the gardener's viewpoint is the lovely Transcaucasian primrose, *P. juliae*. With the possible exception of the primrose and polyanthus it is the most noteworthy of all the primula, for who can estimate the contribution that hybrids from this species have made to the beauty of our gardens? Among them are 'Wanda', with claret-red flowers, 'E. R. Janes', 'Mauve Queen', and the delectable 'Garryarde Guinevere' – the last three from cross-pollination with the common primrose.

Top: *Primula rosea*
Centre: *Primula farinosa*
Above: *Primula*
'Garryarde Guinevere'

Primula scotica

First encounters sometimes remain vivid in the memory, and this is certainly true of my discovery of *P. marginata* growing amongst moss-covered stones in the Maritime Alps. Grey-green, deeply toothed leaves dusted with white powder topped by large lavender-blue flowers combined to make this the most beautiful alpine primula. I grow the plants on a ledge in the rock garden where there is full sun and perfect drainage. The hybrids 'Linda Pope' and 'Holden Clough' are also exceptional. Cuttings made of the woody, rhizomatous stems with a tuft of leaves attached and rooted in sandy compost form a simple method of propagation.

Climatic conditions vary a great deal at high altitudes, depending on which part of the earth's surface the measurement is made. At 10 000 feet (3 000 m) in the European Dolomites there is perpetual snow, whereas at 12 000 feet (3 600 m) in the mountains of western China can be found growing rhododendrons, meconopsis, gentians, and primula. So it would follow that a primula growing at that height in China would probably suffer less severe weather than a primula growing at 6 000 or 7 000 feet (1 800 or 2 100 m) in the European Alps, and yet so many of the Asiatic primula do thrive in gardens throughout the British Isles.

Primula marginata

Primula pulverulenta

For twenty years I worked in a garden with wet clay soil in which primulas grew so well that in the stream garden self-sown seedlings had to be hoed off as weeds. Just to show a proper balance, there are Asiatic primulas so temperamental that only the dedicated specialist can succeed in their cultivation.

There is no doubt that the best display of Candelabra primula I have ever seen were growing in moist soil along both banks of a small stream, with light shade but not root competition from oak trees situated on the south side. *P. beesiana* is typical of the section; the rosy-carmine flowers are carried in whorls up stems which are 30 or more inches (76 cm) in height. The arrangement could be described as a series of wheels gradually decreasing in size from bottom to top; the season, June to July. *P. bulleyana* is a better all-round plant, with candelabra spikes of five or more whorls of orange flowers. Both these species flower from mid-June to August.

A moist soil well-supplied with leaf mould, peat, well-rotted manure or compost is eminently suitable. Light overhead shade prevents the flower colour from fading. Primulas will cross-pollinate with others in the same section in a totally uninhibited way to create a multi-coloured race of hybrids, so division is the only method by which colours are kept true to the parent unless the species are kept isolated.

There are several other species in this section which are worth growing where space permits. *P. cockburniana*, a much dwarfer plant at 12 inches (30 cm) high has flowers of an arresting shade of orange, opening slightly earlier than others in the section. In my experience the species is not a good perennial, but cross-pollination between this and other Candelabra species have produced some delightfully vivid coloured hybrids, usually excellent perennials. I just dot groups of *P. cockburniana* at intervals down the border and leave them to cross naturally, which they do with commendable enthusiasm and efficiency.

P. japonica is robust, almost cabbage-like in growth, but for all that it is extremely handsome when in flower. Originating in Japan, it was brought to this country in 1872, and over the years many forms have been developed with purple, red, rose, and white flowers. It varies in height from 18 to 24 inches (46 to 61 cm), depending on soil conditions. 'Miller's Crimson' and 'Postford White' are fine, sturdy varieties. *P. pulverulenta* is another of the section which, though lovely in its own right, has crossed so freely with *P. cockburniana* that the offspring outshine the parents. 'Red Hugh' is particularly fine, with spikes of orange-red candelabra flowers.

Though most gardens have room for only one or two groups of the taller 'Bog' primula, the distinct, strong-growing 'Giant cowslip', *P. florindae*, is worthy of note. I have actually had this plant growing in the stream bed, and it was unharmed by winter floods. This is not a Candelabra primula and is included in the sub-division Sikkimensis. In June to July, when grown in suitably moist soil, it throws up 3-foot (91-cm) high flower stems, topped by heads of forty or more sweetly scented flowers. The hybrid 'Highdown Orange' offers a colour variation on the yellow theme.

Such is the richness and diversity of form contained within the genus that mastery of the problems attendant on growing species from one group by no means assures success in cultivating all primulas. The Petiolares section contains several lovely species to tempt the unwary, none of them in my experience easy to grow, but I have had enough success to encourage me to keep trying. The lovely *Primula bhutanica* is one such plant. The best example I have seen grows in a Himalayan-type climate on the banks of the River Tay in Scotland. With rainfall in excess of 40 inches (1 m) a year and a mild spring the plants really are a delight. The easiest to grow for me is *P. edgeworthii* from the western Himalayas. The yellow-eyed flowers are a delicate pale mauve around an inner white band. They are held posy-like against the nest of white-powdered leaves. Planted in a vertical crevice between peat blocks, *P. edgeworthii* grew very well, flowering in early April. There the crown of leaves was kept dry while the roots explored the permanently wet soil behind. A crevice between stones on the north face of a rock outcrop would do as well. Alternatively, *P. edgeworthii* will flower well when grown in the alpine house. It is interesting that in one Scottish garden I visited the plant grows in a woodland bed where it flowers superbly. Seed offers the best means of increasing stock for me; I have never dared try the root cuttings recommended by those with larger stocks of the plant than I have ever owned.

P. gracilipes, collected in 1846, is widely distributed in northern China and Tibet at elevations of 13 000 to 16 500 feet (4 000 to 5 000 m). It has flowers of bright pink. *P. sonchifolia* has something of the common primrose charm though with azure-

Top: *Primula edgeworthii*
Centre: *Primula bhutanica*
Above: *Primula gracilipes*

Primula sonchifolia

blue, yellow-eyed flowers. Given a shady place in a leaf-mould soil well-supplied with moisture during growth, *P. sonchifolia* is one of the great challenges to the gardener's skill.

Though the Soldanelloides section includes some difficult species, one of the loveliest, *P. nutans*, needs little persuasion to thrive. I sometimes wonder if some of the primulas which have the reputation of being temperamental are not dying of old age, being only short-lived perennials or even monocarpic. Certainly this is the weakness of *P. nutans*, but as seeds germinate quickly and easily, the replacement of casualties is no problem. It was found by that redoubtable plant-hunting priest, Abbé Delavay, in 1884, about 5 000 feet (1 500 m) above sea level growing in pine woods and open, stony pastures. The place which suits my plants well is in the shade border amongst the rhododendrons. There

from mid-June from amongst the hairy leaves rise stalks 1-foot (39-cm) high ending in clustered heads of nodding, bell-shaped flowers, lavender to violet-blue, which are sweetly scented. It is a flower to bring pure delight to anyone who grows it. A peaty or leaf-mould soil is quite suitable.

Though not easy to grow, *P. reidii* is an exquisite member of the same group, growing only 6 inches (15 cm) high. Discovered on the Kumaon, Western Himalayas, in 1884, growing in amongst stones with roots kept permanently moist by melting snow, it needs care in cultivation. Again, I grow my plants with *P. nutans* in peat soil amongst dwarf rhododendrons. I regularly have to replace casualties, but the seven or eight ivory-white or pale-lavender, bell-shaped sweetly scented flowers are reward enough for my trouble. Grown in the alpine house it would present no problem.

In the section Cortusoides, *P. heucheri folia* is a species which will flourish in a humus-rich soil and a shady position. My plants are soundly perennial and grow in the rhododendron border. Until shoots reappeared in April, I thought the first winter had killed them all, because the top growth dies down completely. Loose heads of dark red flowers open on stems 6 inches (15 cm) high during May and June. Seed is set in abundance, or the plants may be divided to increase stock as growth begins in April.

There are some gardeners, and I am one of them, who find it hard to believe that *P. viali* can really belong in the same family as primroses and polyanthus. Once again it was the Abbé Delavay who found the plants growing in moist meadows on Mount Hee-chan-men in Yunnan but, unfortunately, did not collect seed or plants to send home. Then in 1906 George Forrest, the man who introduced so many good garden plants, rediscovered the species. Though supposedly perennial, a considerable percentage of my plants die after flowering, so it is advisable to sow some seed each year. Often growth is slow to begin; in my garden they flower in mid-June. The flowers, remarkably un-primula-like, show colour in June and July. The scape is variable, about 4 inches (10 cm) long, ending in a dense spike of flowers which are crimson in bud opening to bluish-violet. A plant in bloom looks like an outrageously coloured kniphofia ('Red hot poker'). A group of this primula in flower is a sight to remember. They do well in a partially shaded bed, and in soil which is well drained but not liable to dry out. I bury a layer of well-rotted compost or peat 12 inches (30 cm) below the surface before planting to act as a reservoir of moisture, and I get well-flowered *P. viali*.

Several of the primula species have achieved popularity as greenhouse plants. *P. malacoides*, (Fairy primrose), will flower in late winter and early spring from seed sown at intervals from April to June. The peat-based compost is adequate for seed sowing, and germination takes place about three weeks later in a temperature of 65°F. *P. obconica* has larger blooms, and flowers at the same time and with similar treatment. Both should be grown in a cool temperature of 50°F. as, like most of the species, they will not thrive in a hot, dry atmosphere.

5
Clematis

Clematis and roses are an enduring memory of my childhood years. Though, no doubt, the brush-strokes are bolder, petal colours more vivid in retrospect than they were in reality, both plants still hold a special place in my affections.

There are, in fact, more species of Clematis than of roses, and these are distributed round the temperate regions of the world. The hardy species of gardening interest inhabit China, North America, and Europe. The best-known are the woody climbers, though there are herbaceous forms attractive enough to earn consideration. What surprises me is how little, compared to the rose, clematis figures in poetry, folklore, or garden history. Gerard talks of *Clematis vitalba* as 'Traveller's joy'. The grey-whiskered appearance of the seeds explains, no doubt, the popular name of 'Old man's beard'.

Peculiarly, clematis is included in the buttercup family, which is in itself enough of a contradiction to confuse if a comparison between the two is limited to a visual experience only. The native *C. vitalba*, pleasant enough growing in the hedgerow, is too vigorous for consideration as a garden plant. Not even the fragrance of the double white flowers, reminiscent of almond, compensates for its rampaging persistence.

The European species are of greater merit and importance, particularly the *C. viticella*, which must have been introduced during the sixteenth century, as the blue, red, and double forms are mentioned by writers of the period – first Gerard and then Parkinson – though not with a great deal of enthusiasm for their worth as garden or medicinal plants. *C. viticella* is worthy of note in the historical sense as a parent of some large-flowered garden hybrids. I can remember my father using 'slips' of *C. viticella* as a root-stock on which to graft named varieties that could otherwise be propagated only by means of layers. Gerard also mentioned *C. flammula*, a strong-growing climber up to 10 feet (3 m) high which opens white, sweetly fragrant flowers in late summer. Indeed, it is no surprise that gardeners of an enquiring mind should cross *C. flammula* with *C. viticella* to produce *C.* × 'Rubro marginata', which has reddish-coloured flowers whose only virtue in gardening terms is their fragrance. Possibly, grown over a low wall with sunlight striking through, the flowers may

The author with a beautiful example of *Clematis* 'Jackmanii Superba' outside an Oxfordshire cottage

achieve greater distinction. What I do find very strange is that the lovely *C. alpina* did not reach this country until the late eighteenth century. I first saw the plant in the wild, growing through a 3-foot (0·9-m) high bush of *Rhododendron ferrugineum*. The rose-crimson flower trusses of the 'Alpen Rose' showed the delicate beauty of the blue-petalled clematis to advantage. As the two were growing several thousand feet above sea level on a mountain side, the air of delicacy was an illusion.

C. *alpina* and the several hybrids which have been raised from it are lovely, robust, easily cultivated garden plants. I have grown the white, semi-double-flowered 'White Moth', the pale blue 'Columbine', and 'Ruby' with rose-red blossoms, all excellent but in no way surpassing the species which grows so readily from seed. The hybrids are increased by means of layers or cuttings of semi-ripened shoots. Only a short while after the establishment of *C. alpina* which, to all intents and purposes, had only to slip across the Channel to reach this country, *C. florida* was introduced from Japan. Although the plant is indigenous to China, the Japanese had the species and several garden hybrids bred from it in cultivation for possibly a hundred years before that. Though the species *C. florida* is not reliably hardy outdoors, as the parent of a race of garden hybrids which flower in advance of the other *C. lanuginosa* they are of prime importance. Clematis can be divided into groups, and *C. florida* gives its name to one which includes species and hybrids flowering in early summer. Gardeners in the less-favoured areas will discover that *C. florida* and its hybrids grow better with wall protection. Of the hybrids 'Belle of Woking' with double, pale mauve flowers, and 'Duchess of Edinburgh' with scented, double white blooms are interesting. In 1912 Mr W. Robinson wrote a monograph devoted to clematis in which he denounces all the double-flowered forms as abominable. The single flowers are so perfectly symmetrical that it seems a pity to change them.

Top: *Clematis alpina* 'Columbine'
Above: *Clematis* 'Belle of Woking'

Top right: *Clematis* 'Barbara Dibley'
Centre right: *Clematis* 'Lasurstern'
Below right: *Clematis* 'Vyvyan Pennell'

Not until 1836 did the second species of importance to the hybridist appear. *C. patens* is thought to be of Chinese origin, but was introduced from Japanese gardens by Philip Franz von Siebold. The wild form has white flowers, yet in all the cultivated forms which I have seen the colour ranges from lilac-grey to violet, so possibly the original von Siebold introduction was also a hybrid. This group comes into flower during May and June. They need some pruning to remove weak or dead wood. I also cut back any shoots that are not required to a strong bud, just to ensure that a crop of young wood is available to replace the old stems which are cut away. Of the hybrids, 'Barbara Dibley' has large flowers of pansy-violet with a deep carmine stripe along each petal. 'Lasurstern' is deep lavender-blue with contrasting white stamens, and it frequently carries a second crop of flowers in early autumn. 'Vyvyan Pennell' has full double blooms of deep violet-blue. Those I grew repeatedly blossomed again in August, but with lavender, single flowers. 'The President' is very popular; the purple sepals have a silvery underside.

The hardiest of the three important Chinese 'parent' species to flower, *C. lanuginosa* was also the last to be discovered by Robert Fortune in China. In nature it grows only 6 feet (2 m) high, though with large flowers. Hybrids are more vigorous, and produce blooms measuring 8 inches (20 cm) or more across from June through to October. Prune out dead and weak growth in February to keep the plants well furnished. Though cross-

Clematis 'Nelly Moser'

hybridising among the various groups has blurred familiar characteristics to some extent, the following qualify as *C. lanuginosa/C. patens* offspring. 'Fairy Queen' has very large, pale flesh-pink-coloured flowers with a deeper central bar, which appear in July and August. 'Nelly Moser', one of the most popular of clematis hybrids, has large mauve-pink flowers, each petal relieved with a carmine-pink central bar. It is a climber which should be grown shaded from direct sun or the colour fades to a washed-out magenta. 'W. E. Gladstone' is of sound constitution, a free-flowering climber, the sepals lavender with deep purple anthers.

There are important species which, though contributing improved forms through seedling selection, are not notable or prolific in cross-breeding. *C. montana*, native of the Himalayas and introduced to this country in 1831, is a superb climber. The flowers appear in such profusion in May as completely to hide branches and whatever support they are trained over. Petal blossoms range in colour from pure white to a beautiful rosy-red and measure 2 to 3 inches (5 to 7 cm) across. Propagation is easily achieved by means of cuttings taken at any month from June to February or by means of seed, which is available in large quantities on a mature plant. This is one of the most effective climbing plants for covering unsightly buildings. I have one specimen of the *C. montana* 'Rubens' with rosy-red flowers growing up through an old apple tree. Also worthy of garden-

Clematis 'Nelly Moser'

Clematis montana 'Rubens'

Clematis montana 'Tetrarose'

Clematis macropetala

space is *C. montana* 'Tetrarose', which has lilac-coloured petals with straw-coloured stamens and attractive bronze foliage.

Many of the species are very beautiful, and the gardener whose sole interest is in the large-flowered hybrids with *C. lanuginosa*, *C. viticella*, *C. patens*, or *C. florida* as parents is not fully exploiting the potential of the genus. *C. armandii* is a useful evergreen climber which, though needing wall protection to grow and flower well, is a very distinctive species. The flowers, which open in April, are pure white, fading to rose as they age. 'Apple Blossom' is a lovely form with the white overlaid on pink.

Though *C. indivisa*, a native of New Zealand, is hardy only in milder areas of the country, I grew it in a cold greenhouse for several years and it is exceptionally beautiful. My plant was the form 'Lobata' and produced enormous crops of pure white flowers in the early spring, even though confined in a 10-inch (25-cm) pot.

What a lot of our best garden plants hail from China! *C. macropetala* is a beautiful species discovered in Kansu early this century. The climbing stems are slender and unobtrusive, while the flowers, from 2 to 4 inches (5 to 10 cm) across, bloom in May. The sepals are violet-blue, and the middle is filled with paler-coloured petal-like segments. It could be described as the Chinese counterpart of the European *C. alpina*, and both are restrained enough in growth to be planted on the steeper slopes of a rock garden. I grow the variety 'Markham's Pink' falling

over a large boulder where the rose-coloured flowers look beautiful against the moss-covered stone. The seed heads, which are covered in feathery tails, are themselves decorative. Seed sown immediately it is fully ripe makes an easy method of increasing stock of the species. Hybrids are best propagated by means of semi-ripe cuttings in June, July, or August.

There are two yellow-flowered species that I have enjoyed growing. The first is *C. orientalis*, which grows wild in northern Asia. Popularly known as the 'Orange-peel clematis', the orange-yellow curved petals are cupped like a partially segmented tangerine. The flowers measure approximately 2 inches (5 cm) across, have a delicate but quite discernible fragrance, and open during August and September. As the buds develop on young growth of the current season, the previous season's shoots can be cut away, as they quite frequently die each autumn anyway. I do all pruning as growth begins in late spring when it is obvious which shoots are, in fact, dead. New stock can easily be raised by sowing seed into general-purpose seed compost in March.

The other yellow-flowered species, *C. tangutica*, is the one I prefer. Although both are very desirable garden plants, *C. tangutica* is of such an easygoing disposition, and flowers so abundantly from July onwards, that it just achieves the higher rating. New plants grow so readily from seed that it costs only effort to stock a large garden. I have used seedlings as ground cover in a limestone rock garden, to grow over shrubs in a mixed border, and had them masking a steep bank in crisp yellow flowers, then later with the silvered seed heads. First introduced from China in 1898 (compared to *C. orientalis*, which appeared in 1730), *C. tangutica* is a comparative newcomer which gained official recognition with an Award of Garden Merit in 1934.

We enjoy the results of creative effort by previous generations of gardeners and hybridists. The first large-flowered species

Above left: *Clematis orientalis*
Above: *Clematis macropetala* 'Snowbird'

Top right: *Clematis* 'Jackmanii Rubra'
Below right: *Clematis integrifolia*

introduced into cultivation flowered only meagrely, so nurserymen started crossing between species to see if hybrid vigour improved the yield of flowers and colour variation.

The first recorded clematis cross was between *C. viticella* and *C. integrifolia*. This occurred at the Pine-apple Nursery belonging to Mr Henderson at St John's Wood in 1835. Henderson's cross is known as *C. × eriostemon* 'Hendersonii'. In 1858 Messrs Jackman of Woking made a double cross using *C. lanuginosa* as the seed parent and the pollen of both *C. × eriostemon* 'Hendersonii' and of *C. viticella* 'Atrorubens'. The famous *C. × Jackmanii* was one of many resulting seedlings.

So closely were Jackmans associated with clematis that in my early gardening years I thought there was a race of purple flowering plants called not clematis but jackmanii! Certainly the large, violet-coloured, velvet-textured blooms of the Jackmanii are more frequently a feature in gardens than any other species or variety. There seems to be no discernible genetic reason why the yellow-flowered species cannot be crossed with other species and hybrids. Perhaps those who, like myself, have tried in a haphazard way to effect a union between, say, *C. tangutica* and 'Perle

d'Azure', or *C. tangutica* and 'La France' without success, gave up too easily. Possibly in a few years a whole new race of large-flowered, buttercup-yellow-bloomed hybrids will add further contrast to the violets, blues, reds, and whites gracing our gardens.

All clematis I have seen growing wild under natural conditions favoured a habitat amongst shrubs and an alkaline soil. A good basic rule when choosing a place and preparing a soil for clematis would be roots in shade, tops in sun. Lime is not an absolute essential, at least with strong-growing species like *C. montana* or vigorous hybrids. These grew in the very acid soil which I gardened for twenty years, but did not show the robust good health of similar plants established in a magnesium limestone-based loam. Avoid soils which are liable to waterlog or those which become bone dry in the summer. Even on what are termed 'good' soils I still prepare the site for planting. Dig out the existing soil 15 inches (38 cm) deep to leave a hole measuring 2 feet (0·6 m) across. I lose the subsoil in the vegetable garden, then make up the difference by mixing the top soil which is left with compost or horticultural peat, plus a generous dusting of bone meal. This preparation is advisable on average soil, but essential on badly drained clay or light sandy soil. Break up any hard pan at the base of the hole by forking in a shovel full of moist peat or well-rotted compost. The problem of drainage on heavy soils can, to some extent, be overcome by high planting – that is, raising the level by means of paving slabs, bricks, or stone blocks by, say, 10 inches (25 cm) above that of the surrounding soil.

Time of planting depends on the location of the garden, though late April or early May is my preference. By buying plants which are growing in pots the root disturbance is minimal, and with care there is no check to progress at all. Clematis do not like the soil rammed hard around the roots, so I do all the firming down with fingers or only very gently with my boot heel to leave the top of the root ball level with the soil surface. This leaves room for a 4-inch (10-cm) mulch of peat or rotted compost: an

Top: *Clematis* 'The President'
Above: *Clematis* 'Jackmanii Superba'

excellent way of keeping roots cool and moist. During the first three months after planting out keep the soil well watered, not just round the stem but for 18 inches (46 cm) either side to encourage the roots to spread out and establish. Usually pot-grown plants are tied in to a supporting cane. I leave this in, then just fasten it back to the trellis or whatever the stems are to be trained over. Some years ago I was given a present of the lovely *texensis* hybrid, 'Gravetye Beauty', which has flowers like lapageria. In trying to remove the cane I broke the stem, and the whole plant died. Make sure the stem is held firm, then, as growth starts, train out the young shoots which are very brittle and easily damaged and tie them in position. Each spring after planting I mulch the soil over the roots with well-rotted manure, compost, or peat, and a 4-inch (10-cm) potful of bone meal added to each 2 gallon (9-litre) bucketful of the mulching material. The clematis grown in tubs as patio decoration are given the mulch in spring, then a liquid feed at three-week intervals during the growing season. Another favourite is the lavender-coloured 'Countess of Lovelace'. This has double flowers in the summer and single flowers in the autumn.

Clematis can be used to decorative advantage in various places in the garden. As tub- or container-grown specimens for terrace or patio, they will grow perfectly well in the John Innes No. 3 compost. Suitable varieties to grow in containers would be early flowering, any of the *C. alpina* or *C. macropetala*. The following varieties continue the succession of flowering:

'Corona' – light purple-pink, growing 7 feet (2 m) high;
'Miss Bateman' – white, 6 feet (1·8 m) high;
'The President' – rich purple, 9 feet (2·7 m) high;
'John Warren' – dark pink, 9 feet (2·7 m) high;
'Jackmanii Superba' – dark purple, 9 feet (2·7 m) high.

Clematis 'Countess of Lovelace'

Pruning consists of cleaning out dead and weak growth, except for 'Jackmanii Superba' which should be cut hard back to a good growth bud near soil level.

Each spring carefully remove the top inch or two (2·5 or 5 cm) of soil from the container and top up with more John Innes No. 3 compost. Pruning and careful training in of the young shoots will produce a well-furnished plant, and a spectacular display of flowers. Regular watering and feeding are the other essentials.

For growing through trees or over large walls the stronger-growing species are the best value. Soil preparation is particularly important, as the soil at the base of a tree or foot of a wall is often dry and impoverished.

Among suitable varieties are all forms of *C. montana*. These are excellent and need little pruning. 'Highdown', a variety of *C. vedrariensis*, grows 12 to 18 feet (3·6 to 5·4 m) high, and opens myriads of small pink flowers in May. Again, it needs little pruning. 'Comtesse de Bouchaud', growing 12 to 15 feet (3·6 to 4·5 m) with mauve-pink flowers in August, is decorative but needs hard pruning to maintain vigour. Prune back to a bud just above the base of the previous season's growth. I like to keep all flowering shoots on this variety growing from as near soil level as possible.

When clematis are grown on walls, some sort of supporting trellis or wire will be necessary. Wood or plastic-covered wire is suitable, and is best fixed on wooden battens which provide a clearance from the wall of an inch or so to allow air circulation. Prepare the soil as described, then step the roots out from the base of the wall at least 10 inches (25 cm). No matter how well the soil is made up, that immediately alongside the wall is so dry that the roots struggle to grow. Stepping the roots out solves the problem.

As far as simplifying and summing up the pruning is concerned, most years early-flowering species and varieties – for example, *C. montana* – will need only a general clean-up of dead stems and weak growth. They can be pruned harder if necessary when they grow too large for the space allotted to them. The May-to-June flowering species and varieties, *C. patens*, *C. florida* and *C. lanuginosa* may have the old flowering shoots cut back as the blossoms fade. I also like to thin out over-dense growth and dead or weak branches where necessary in February. Finally, those species which flower on young growths of the current season – Jackmanii is a good example – should be cut right back to within two buds of the old wood. Left unpruned, the plants grow bare at the base, and the flowers open out of sight on the top branches.

There are so many hybrids on offer that I have made no attempt to list them. Which ones to grow must be a personal choice in terms of the site and type of soil available and the flower colour desired. All other considerations aside, clematis are such superb climbing plants that no effort put in to growing them really well will be wasted.

Clematis 'Comtesse de Bouchaud'

6
Irises

Would that all the plants which grace our gardens were named so appropriately! For Iris was one of the Oceanides, goddess of the multi-hued rainbow, and favoured attendant of Juno. Indeed, there could hardly be a more descriptive name, for the iris flowers borrow all the colours of the rainbow. Anyone who doubts this should walk through a garden of modern bearded iris in full bloom. Under the June sunlight the petals of the flowers show innumerable shades and variations of colour.

The Greeks planted iris on the graves of their dead, for just as Mercury conducted the souls of departed males to heaven, so Iris supposedly performed a like service for the women.

The three leaf petals represent valour, wisdom, and faith. Adopted as his device on the Second Crusade by Louis VII of France, iris flowers soon became celebrated as the Fleur de Louis, adapted to Fleur de Luce, and later to Fleur de Lis – the lily flower: not just a change of name but a change of genus when the iris became a lily.

Of the two hundred or more species of iris only two are native to this country: *Iris foetidissima* and *I. pseudacorus*. *I. foetidissima* is known as 'Stinking Gladwin' or the 'Roast-beef plant'. It is also descriptively referred to as 'Spurge-wort', because substances in the fresh root-stock were much in demand when purging was a popular medicinal cure-all, and is an interesting garden plant.

This species is a slow-growing perennial with purple or pale yellow flowers appearing in early summer. These are followed in due season by a dark brown seed capsule which is full of scarlet-red seeds, much sought after for use in dried flower arrangements. Any reasonably moist and fertile garden soil will suit this species. Propagation is easily effected by means of seed or by division.

I. pseudacorus, (Yellow flag), which grows along the margins of ponds and rivers over much of the British Isles, merits a place in the garden. The yellow flowers, carried on stems 3 feet (0·9 m) high, show up best against a dark background. There are different forms with flower colours which are merely variations on a yellow theme. In one herbal which I read recently the ground-up seeds are suggested as a substitute for coffee. I have

Iris pseudacorus growing on
the banks of a Devon marsh

not yet plucked up courage to try the infusion. The form
'Variegata' is a most striking foliage plant: the leaves in spring
are striped yellow.

The common iris, *I. germanica*, lays claim to being the oldest
plant in cultivation, though I question how this could be proved
or disproved. In his discourse on the medicinal properties of
plants, Pliny describes with great exactitude how the roots which
contain these properties should be dug up. *I. germanica* is a
strong-growing species which shows extensive variations in form
and flower colour. The most notable form is *florentina*, cultivated
since the times of ancient Greece. This is the source of orris,
which is made from the violet-scented, powdered rootstock used
for hundreds of years in the perfumery trade. Nowadays, *I.
pallida* has largely replaced it for this purpose. *I. germanica
florentina* is still grown in commercial quantities in Italy, Egypt,
Iran, and India. For toiletry preparations the roots need to be
well dried before the violet scent is apparent.

Before becoming involved in the description of the best species of iris available for cultivation in the garden, let us consider first the characteristics of the iris. There are two distinct types of root systems. One grows from bulbs or bulb-like corms and contains some very lovely spring-flowering species. The other group has a stout stem-like root – rhizomatous or fibrous. Fortunately, most of the species are hardy outdoors in this country, and by careful selection the garden can provide iris in flower for eight or nine months of the year. In one respect they are easily recognisable: that is by the shape of the flowers, which throughout the species are remarkably similar, with three outer, reflexed petals, often bearded, and three inner, smaller, upright petals known as standards.

Though iris are divided for the convenience of the botanically minded into eleven groups, for my purpose they are better considered in terms of flowering times. The season begins with *I. unguicularis*, whose flowering period in favoured areas can, by judicious selection of varieties, be extended from November to early spring. As would be expected of a plant whose natural home is the eastern Mediterranean, *I. unguicularis* (syn. *I. stylosa*) needs a well-drained soil and the sunniest position which the garden affords. In my last garden a bed made up under the overhanging eaves of the house on a south-facing wall proved excellent. To make certain that the drainage was correct I mixed in a generous dressing of sharp sand until the soil must have been poor to the point of sterility. In this arid medium, encouraged by an annual dressing of leaf mould mixed with dried seaweed fertiliser, the iris produced a succession of flowers which made even grey February tolerable. Recently a friend introduced me to a variety called 'Walter Butt' which carried blooms of palest lilac, in my opinion inferior to the type. A feature of species and hybrids is the delicate fragrance of the flowers – like sun-warmed violets. All grow to about 20 inches (51 cm) tall.

Of the bulbous species which can be persuaded into flower in late winter and early spring, I have only appreciative praise. In

Below left: *Iris unguicularis*
Below: *Iris danfordiae*

Iris winogradowii

Iris reticulata

most gardens there is a sheltered corner which gathers every ray of sunshine as a miser hoards gold; this is the place to select for *I. histrioides*. The flowers, which appear before the leaves, are large, vivid blue, the fall petal traced with an orange-crested beard. Frequently I have had this species flowering through a carpet of snow with unblemished petals.

I. danfordiae is a yellow-petalled counterpart to the blue *I. histrioides*, and is not so reliably perennial. The bulbs flower well the first year after planting, then divide into a multitude of bulblets none large enough to produce more than leaves in subsequent seasons. They are so lovely that I consider money spent on new stock each year a good investment.

The best-known species, available in several different colour forms, is the delectable, sweet-scented *I. reticulata*. In the type species which I grow the petals are deep violet-blue. There are so many varieties, including hybrids with *I. histrioides* that it is almost a case of being spoiled for choice. 'J. S. Dijt', red-purple, 'Cantab', light blue, and 'Harmony', sky-blue, are a choice selection. Also a particular favourite of mine is the species with lemon-yellow flowers, *I. winogradowii*, which grows wild in the Caucasus.

Given a well-drained soil with a top dressing of seaweed fertiliser, bone meal, or meat, fish and bone meal, both *I. histrioides* and *I. reticulata* maintain good flowering colonies. All the bulbous, spring-blooming irises described grow 4- to 6-inch (10- to 15-cm) high flowering stems, but leaf growth extends to 12 inches (30 cm) or more. Plant the bulbs 3 to 4 inches (8 to 10 cm) deep during autumn.

There is another group of spring-flowering, so-called 'bulbous-rooted' irises which need special cultivation – the Juno. All species in the group require good drainage and a hot, sun-baked position. In northern gardens they are best accommodated in a raised frame filled with a sandy compost. During very cold weather the frame can be kept closed, and again in summer when the bulbs are ripening the glass will protect the plants from

Iris bucharica

excess rain. The easiest to grow of this group, *I. bucharica* has a 12-inch (30 cm) high leaf fan. Curiously shaped yellow and white flowers open during early spring. *I. albo-marginata* has attractive grey-blue flowers. The bulbs are planted in September 4 inches (10 cm) deep in a well-drained soil.

Flowering later in spring, usually early to mid-May, *I. douglasiana* and *I. innominata* of the Apogon group represent an entire change in character. Their leaves are evergreen, growing from root-like underground stems. Flowers on 12-inch (30-cm) stems vary in colour from pink, lilac, yellow to white, with the petal veins in contrasting shades of the base tint. Any good garden soil which does not either become waterlogged in winter

Below left: Juno species growing at the Royal Botanic Garden, Kew
Below: *Iris albo-marginata*

Tall bearded irises in full bloom
in a Nottinghamshire garden

or dry out completely in summer will grow both species successfully. Increase by seed or division is easily achieved.

The bearded iris is the most easily recognisable and familiar
of all the clan. Indeed, it is of some consolation to anyone who
tries to unravel the very complex iris lineage that in all parts –
root, leaf, and flower – they are so distinctive. The first specialist
hybridiser of bearded, flag or German iris was a Frenchman,
Lémon, who began selective cross-pollination using several
species in the early 1800s. *I. germanica* is not, as I assumed,
responsible for the immense range of tall, intermediate and
dwarf May- and June-flowering bearded forms listed by nurserymen at present. The real ancestors are *I. variegata*, *I. pallida*,
I. trojana, and, more recently, *I. chamaeiris*, which has been used
to produce smaller, more manageable varieties.

When comparing the small-flowered, rather funereal-
coloured blues and purples of earlier varieties (the main virtue of
which was the ability to survive in any soil or situation) with the
rainbow-hued hybrids of today, the transformation is barely
credible. Whenever the hybridist embarks on an expanding
breeding programme with ever-larger, more extravagantly
coloured flowers as the sole purpose, inevitably, other less
advantageous characteristics appear. Modern hybrids are not so
hardy, nor do they adapt so readily to a wide range of soils or
situations. Flowers are enormous and multi-hued, the petals
crimped and ruffled, but they are carried on tall stems which are
easily damaged by strong winds or heavy rain.

The dwarf iris, from crosses between the tall sorts and *I.
chamaeiris*, are better value for the small garden. There still
remains the challenge of breeding to achieve a race of bearded iris

with the hardiness of 'Kochii' and the petal colours of 'Mulberry Rose'. Those wishing to grow a selection of modern varieties will need to choose from the hundreds available, as new ones are being introduced each year. Fortunately, the early hybrids from *I. pallida* × *variegata* are preserved to enjoy a new popularity as labour-saving garden plants.

Bearded iris are plants of the sunshine, and will not flower unless they are fully exposed in a south-facing border. A well-drained soil is another essential, preferably alkaline in reaction. In my last garden I had of necessity to grow several hundred new varieties of bearded iris in a heavy, lime-free, clay soil. Working in heavy dressings of limestone chippings improved drainage and the lime content enough to make conditions acceptable to the iris, which grew and flowered well.

The time of planting is important, and should be carried out just before the new roots develop. One of the characteristics of the bearded iris is that after flowering a whole new root system starts growing, so lifting, dividing, and replanting should be done as the last flower dies in early July. Choose young, vigorous, disease-free roots (rhizomes), each with a good fan of leaves. Before planting I shorten the leaf growth by half to prevent them being blown about by the wind. Adjust the depth of planting so the root (rhizome) is left exposed on the surface. Once planting is completed I dust the soil around the root with basic slag or superphosphate, which seems to encourage strong root growth. Dividing and replanting can be carried out at three- or four-year intervals, as the roots get overgrown and flower only sparsely. A dusting of fertiliser containing superphosphate and potash each year in April is all the supplementary feeding that this group of iris requires.

The Apogon group, which includes the spring-flowering American species iris, *I. douglasiana* and *I. innominata* previously described, also harbours notable summer-flowering species. One of the easiest to accommodate, requiring soil which does not dry out in summer, is *I. sibirica*, native of Europe and Asia, and certainly cultivated in this country before the seventeenth century. This is a splendid garden plant which, once installed, asks only to be left undisturbed. The grass-like foliage is a foil to broad-leaved hosta or primula. My choice of varieties carry flowers on stems protruding well above the foliage: 'Dreaming Spire', a dark blue; 'Sea Shadows', a fine mid-blue; and 'Anniversary', white.

One of the inexplicable complications of iris classification is the way in which easily grown species share the same group as those which are rare and difficult to grow. Included in the Laevigatae group with the easygoing American and European species are two lovely Japanese species brought to this country midway through the last century. First to arrive was *I. kaempferi*, which in the quality of its velvet-textured flowers rivals the orchid. In order to discover the best conditions for growing this rather temperamental beauty I tried planting one in shallow water, another in moist soil at the pool edge, and a third in a specially prepared moisture-retentive bed. I removed the soil,

Iris 'Curlew' (Intermediate bearded)

Below: *Iris* 'One Desire' (Tall bearded)
Top right: *Iris sibirica* 'Sea Shadows'
Below right: *Iris sibirica* 'Anniversary'

which was lime-free, to a depth of 18 inches (46 cm), spread a thick layer of well-rotted manure in the hole, then replaced the soil, mixing in more rotted manure at the same time. The planting (from containers) was carried out in mid-May. Pool-edge planting needs no special soil preparation, but those grown in shallow water are best grown in the open-work plastic baskets specially designed to keep the crown dry. The varieties 'Rose Queen', 'Purple Splendour' and those listed under 'Higo' hybrids are amongst the loveliest flowers which ever graced our gardens. They grow to around 30 inches (76 cm) in a lime-free soil.

The other Japanese introduction, *I. laevigata*, will grow well if planted beside a garden pool or stream. In one garden I know the lavender-blue and white-flowered hybrids luxuriate in a bed of peaty soil, kept well-watered during very dry weather. The leaves of this species are broader paler green than those of *I. kaempferi*, particularly those of the pastel-shaded flowered forms. The species introduced from Japan in 1856 has broad-

petalled, clear blue flowers. In the form *I. albo-purpurea* the blue is mottled and suffused with white, which, though very attractive, is less pleasing to me than the pure white 'Alba'. Some of the best examples of *I. laevigata* hybrids are to be found in the Bagatelle garden in Paris. The less common *I. laevigata* 'Variegata' has the bonus of attractive foliage to complement the violet-blue flowers. Though closely enough related to *I. kaempferi* for crosses to have been made between the species, neither *I. laevigata* nor the hybrids seem to scorn a soil which contains lime.

The species *I. ochroleuca* (the Butterfly iris) is a worthy garden plant. The leaves are over 3 feet (0·9 m) long, and a succession of cream white flowers are borne in late June.

Why *I. xiphioides* enjoys the popular name of 'English iris' when it hails from the Pyrenees is one of those unexplained garden mysteries. Merchants trading from Bristol imported the bulbs, which established themselves so readily that they became a common garden feature. Eventually the bulbs were exported back to Holland. Could this possibly explain the popular name

Below left: *Iris laevigata* 'Variegata'
Below: *Iris ochroleuca*

Above: *Iris laevigata* 'Apaisie'
Above right: *Iris laevigata* 'Tamura'

Iris xiphium 'Yellow Queen'

English iris? Soil prepared by trenching and manuring seems to suit this iris. For six years I planted the bulbs 4 inches (10 cm) deep along a trench that in the previous years had grown sweet peas, and they flowered exceedingly well. The type colour is blue, though mixed varieties give the best display.

Useful also as a cut flower *I. xiphium*, 'Spanish iris', is closely related to English iris, though flowering slightly earlier. They are available in a wide range of colours, and grow in well-drained soil and full sun. Their height is between 18 and 24 inches (46 and 61 cm). The 'Dutch iris' (a hybrid between *I. xiphium* and *I. tingitana*) is reported as being a selected form of the Spanish iris. These flower early, and include amongst the blue and violet some fine yellow-flowered varieties – for example, 'Yellow Queen'.

I. tingitana, a native of Morocco, is the first to flower. The popular 'Wedgwood', so excellent for forcing, is reputed to be a variety of this species – which surprises me, for I have always bought it as Dutch iris.

Next into bloom come the Dutch *I. xiphium* hybrids such as 'Yellow Queen' and 'Excelsior', followed by the lovely *I. filifolia*, then the Spanish and British 'Celestial', 'Sweet Scented', 'King of the Blues', and 'Leviathan'.

The earliest varieties are potted up in August, then watered and stood outside in a cool place until moved under glass in early October. In a temperature of 50°F. flowers are ready for cutting in late November. The main crop bulbs are potted up in September and stored in a cool place until they are moved inside in late November. They are kept at a temperature of 48°F. until the flower buds show, rising to 55°F., and cutting can usually commence in February. Further stocks are moved in to keep up a succession throughout the winter. The main requirement for success is to keep the bulbs well-supplied with moisture without letting the soil become stagnant.

The range and variety of iris is immense, some being tiny enough to grow in company with the smallest rock plants. Certainly, I would miss those which grow and flower in my own garden.

7
Dahlias

The cultivated forms of dahlia show remarkable variability in flower shape and colour. Indeed, anyone who has grown dahlias in any quantity for several years will have discovered how a variety can produce, without any visible stimulus, a flower or flowers of entirely different colour. The change is usually, but not invariably, in colour only; the shape remains that of the parent variety. Even bearing this instability in mind, it comes as a surprise to those gardeners who consider the art and craft of gardening to have their origins in the British Isles to learn that when the dahlia was discovered four hundred years ago in Mexico by Spanish invaders, it was already being grown by the Aztecs.

One way in which to appreciate how dramatic and far-reaching are the changes which have been made by hybridisation is to compare a lovely wild species like *Dahlia merckii* with one of the large, flamboyant entries in the Giant-flowered Class at any dahlia show. They are in truth four hundred years apart.

The first dahlias were introduced to Europe in 1789 when the Botanic Gardens in Mexico sent seeds to the Royal Gardens in Madrid. One of the seedlings flowered in the following year, and the genus was named *Dahlia* in honour of the Swedish botanist Dahl. Such are the vagaries, the happy chances on which immortality is built. The Aztecs who grew dahlias take second place to a Swedish botanist whose only claim to honour was that he studied under Linnaeus. But for the dahlia, no doubt, Dr Dahl would long ago have been forgotten.

At first, encouraged by the plant's forming potato-like tubers, hopes were kindled that the dahlia would prove to be a new vegetable. Having tasted roast dahlia tubers, I would agree that though non-poisonous they are certainly disagreeably unappetising.

Modern students have identified the first species introduced as *D. pinnata*, *D. coccinea* and *D. rosea*. Though these early species were not of spectacular floral merit, even the first seedlings to flower showed the family instability when some of them developed semi-double flowers. Possibly seed from what were purported to be species were, in fact, hybrids arising from crosses made between the species.

Hybrid dahlias being taken
to a Mexican market

A collection of seeds sent directly from Mexico to Europe in 1804 produced a very variable crop of seedlings with single and semi-double flowers. The first fully double blooms were bred by M. Donkelaar in 1812. By 1814 botanists working in the Botanic Garden at Louvain had produced the first white dahlia, several large-flowered doubles and dwarf plants, which were to give rise to those most popular dahlias, the versatile 'Coltness hybrids'. In the period between 1814 and 1828 stock of the new races of dahlias were imported to Britain from Europe, and the gardeners of that era quickly recognised the potential of the flower which provides colour in the garden until October.

Unlike the rose, rhododendron, and many popular flowers which take several years to reach flowering size, dahlias can be grown from seed to maturity in one growing season. Even considering the speed with which new generations of hybrid dahlia can be produced, it is incredible just how many varieties were being offered in catalogues by 1820: doubles, semi-doubles, singles, and the first bicolours in almost the comprehensive range of colours that gardeners expect of present-day nurseries. The dahlia had, indeed, become, according to London's *Encyclopaedia of Gardening*, 'the most fashionable flower' in these

Above left: *Dahlia* 'Corina'
(Single-flowered)
Above: *Dahlia* 'Omo'
(Single-flowered)

islands. Though the first three-quarters of the nineteenth century showed a progressive development in the shape and quality of the flowers, it was along broadly established lines. For example, the earliest Pompon dahlias were ill proportioned, the small flower perched on the end of a 3- to 4-foot (0·9 to 1·2 m) stem. Selective breeding reduced the stem length to correspond proportionately with the size of the flower. Varieties increased to the extent that in 1841 Harrison's Nursery listed over a thousand double-flowered varieties, presumably of the form which subsequently would be classified as formal Decorative dahlias.

The next development in the hybridising field came when a Mr Van der Burgh took delivery of a parcel of plants from Mexico. Nearly all had died *en route*, but fortunately one, a dahlia tuber, had survived. This was planted and grew to produce a scarlet flower with long-quilled petals. Subsequently this variation, named *D. juarezii*, was cross-pollinated with existing varieties to produce a new class – the Cactus dahlia. When a new species of distinctly different form is imported, a great impetus is given to the propagation of hybrids, and this was the result once the quilled, petalled *D. juarezii* presented itself.

Cactus dahlias crossed with show or Decorative dahlias generated sufficient variation to warrant the addition of several new classes to the list, including the Paeony-flowered, which is a direct result of the cross between Cactus and the ball-type show dahlia.

Dahlias are classified for show purposes according to flower shape: 'Single-flowered', with a single outer ring of petals around an open central disc; 'Anemone-flowered', which have the ring or rings of flattened petals surrounding a central boss of shorter, tubular petals – rather like a quilled pincushion; 'Collerette', with the ring of outer petals complemented by a ring of shorter, inner petals often of a contrasting colour; 'Paeony-flowered' – less fashionable now – with a looser, less regular petal formation, precisely resembling the border Paeonia. 'Decorative' dahlias are full double with flat or slightly incurving petals in a perfectly globular head. 'Ball' dahlias are full double

Dahlia 'Opal' (Ball)

Above: *Dahlia* 'Fascination'
(Paeony-flowered)
Above right: *Dahlia* 'La Cierva'
(Collerette)
Right: *Dahlia* 'Kidd's Climax'
(Giant Decorative)

Below: *Dahlia* 'Honey'
(Anemone-flowered)
Below right: *Dahlia* 'Winston Churchill'
(Miniature Decorative)

Above: *Dahlia* 'Salmon Symbol'
(Medium Semi-Cactus)
Left: *Dahlia* 'Doris Day'
(Small-flowered Cactus)

Below: *Dahlia pinnata*

and spherical in outline. 'Pompon' have spherical heads no more than 2 inches (5 cm) in diameter. 'Cactus' dahlias have petals which are rolled and narrow, so producing a spiky effect.

There are intermediate and miscellaneous varieties which do not fit into any of the groups, but they add a fascinating piquancy to the growing of the unpredictable but never boring dahlia. In time there may be a blue dahlia, a scented dahlia, or – dare we hope? – a hardy dahlia.

There is one question which emerges which I find particularly interesting and worth investigation. How many of the true species are really true species and not garden or natural hybrids? How fascinating and informative an Aztec dahlia grower's garden diary of the early 1600s would be to read now! We do know that the Indians called the dahlias 'Acocotli' or 'hollow pipes', and used the stems as aqueducts in farm-irrigation systems. Mexicans call the plant 'Cocoxochitl', and use the extract from the roots as a tonic. Dahlia tubers yield a pure laevulose – the popular name is 'diabetic sugar' – which is sweet and pleasant to taste; it is material which was frequently prescribed for consumptive and diabetic patients. Presumably the dahlia was of such medicinal and economic value that it can be readily assumed that the natives were assiduous in its cultivation long before Cortés or his minions disrupted their way of life. The students of chromosomes and cell tissue may in time unravel the mystery of the parentage of modern dahlias, though with clues four to five hundred years old they are late in starting.

Garden dictionaries list about a dozen species, with qualifications and synonyms. Most of those listed are presumably not in cultivation or they would be used in hybridisation to create new varieties. *D. coccinea*, with dark brown stems and vivid scarlet flowers on stalks 36 inches (91 cm) high, has a place in history as one of the first species to be introduced. A very old variety which is still a first-class garden plant, 'Bishop of Llandaff' shows *coccinea* ancestry in both flower and stem colour. *D. pinnata*, as already mentioned, was the first dahlia to be brought to this country. The flowers on this species are large, bluish-red, and

Below: *Dahlia coccinea*
Below right: *Dahlia* 'Bishop of Llandaff' at Burford House Gardens, Tenbury Wells

carried on 3-foot (0·9-m) stems. *D. juarezii*, with bright scarlet blooms, is the ancestral Cactus dahlia, and is reputedly a hybrid derived from *D. popenovii* with similarly coloured but less quilled petals. *D. merckii*, in fact, has proved almost hardy: in some gardens plants which have been left outdoors four or five years have shown no ill effects. A mature plant of this age in full bloom is a lovely sight. The single, lilac-petalled flowers have a contrasting central boss of yellow and purple, and are certainly worthy of a place in the garden on their own merit.

D. variabilis is now reported to be synonymous with *D. rosea*. That both are names used to describe many different forms matters little, as the primary parent of garden dahlias, their offspring, like Abraham's, are as numerous as the sands of the sea shore.

D. scapigera, which I found in a pine forest in the west of Mexico, is the smallest of the species. On the other hand, *D. imperialis* and *D. excelsa* are enormous plants with stems up to 20 feet (6 m) high. Neither appears to have figured in the hybridists' stud book, which is fortunate, for a step ladder would be required by anyone who wished to admire the flowers. In the absence of new species progress in hybridisation will be restricted within the lines already established.

There are three methods of propagating dahlias. The most obvious is by sowing seed, which is very unpredictable. Even when the seed is reported as collected from a species I have on occasions discovered some variation in seedlings. Could this, I wonder, indicate that the dahlia is infertile unless cross-pollinated? Self-sterility would, in fact, seem a reasonable assumption. To produce plants identical with the parent, all

Left and below: *Dahlia merckii* growing wild in central Mexico
Right: *Dahlia scapigera*

cultivars (usually a form which has been developed in the garden as a result of cultivation, and not known in the wild) have to be propagated by means of cuttings or division.

Division of the swollen root tubers is widely practised, particularly amongst amateur growers. Usually a strong, healthy root when carefully dissected will yield up to five potential new plants, which is enough to supply the needs of the average-sized garden. Before dividing up the root which has been stored in a frost-free place over the winter, I box them up in a peat compost, then spray lightly overhead with water just to swell the tubers. In the area where the swollen root joins the old stem are dormant buds, which begin to swell as the roots take up moisture. An essential requirement of success with tuber division is that each section should contain at least one of these young growths or eye buds, as they are known. Without this the tuber will just shrivel and die. Late April or early May is the best time to divide the roots, which are then either potted or planted in deep boxes using peat- or loam-based compost. Which compost is used makes no difference so long as there is a food supply readily available for the divisions to strike roots into. Keep them well-watered until early June when all fear of frost is gone, and the flourishing young plants can go out into the open garden. The divisions will grow on to flower in the autumn and also supply tubers fit for storing and subsequent division the following spring.

Cuttings, as with division, give rise to plants identical with the parent. There is something immensely satisfying about taking cuttings: the process of turning one plant into several never loses its appeal. The tubers, whether bought from the nursery or those lifted from the garden the previous autumn, are

Left and above: Geoffrey Smith
admires a fine specimen of
Dahlia imperialis in south Mexico

placed in deep trays or similar containers bedded in compost
which is free draining. The peat-based mixtures with added sand
are quite suitable. Bury the roots so that the point where tuber
and stem join is just exposed. Water them in, then stand the
boxes in a warm, light place. When the young shoots which
develop are 3 to 4 inches (8 to 10 cm) high, cut them off with a
razor-sharp knife and root them in a mixture of peat and sand.
Given a little bottom heat the cuttings will be ready for potting
off in a fortnight. Some growers advise pulling the cuttings from
the parent tuber, as these root more readily. In my experience
this method greatly reduces the number of cuttings thrown by
each root tuber.

The peat-based composts or the John Innes No. 1 potting
compost will guarantee that the young plants maintain balanced
growth until they go out into the garden during late May.

Raising new dahlias from seed is an experience to be enjoyed,
particularly when dealing with the Decorative or Cactus

varieties. No one can predict precisely what sort of flowers the seedlings will eventually produce. They will all flower, and amongst the very average blooms there may be one or more of such outstanding merit that it achieves a name and distinction on the show bench.

Bedding dahlias are more predictable, and many thousands of 'Coltness' and similar dwarf varieties are raised annually for use in summer bedding schemes. Seed should be sown under glass at any time from February to April, depending on how well the greenhouse is heated. For April sowings usually no supplementary heat is needed – except in very cold, freak conditions such as those experienced in late April 1981. Sow the seed into a standard peat or loam compost in the usual way, then cover the trays with newspaper to conserve heat and moisture. Once the seedlings are big enough to handle they can be pricked off and grown on in exactly the same way as for cuttings.

A bed of dahlias in full bloom in September sunlight is a pleasing sight. Like any other garden plant they will flower all the better in well-prepared soil. Choose a warm, sheltered site in full sun: as one would expect with plants from Mexico they appreciate warmth and dislike cold winds. In order to make certain that the soil is in good condition I dig in heavy dressings of rotted manure or similar organic matter at some time during the winter. Then, ten days before planting I lightly fork in 2 oz per square yard (57 g per 0·8 square m) of a complete fertiliser just to give the young dahlia a proper start. How far apart the plants are spaced depends on the variety: about 18 inches (46 cm) each way for bedding types, an average of 24 inches (61 cm) for the rest – except the giant varieties which in the course of a single season grow 4 or 5 feet (1·2 or 1·5 m) by as much across. Water each plant in, then make sure that each stem is tied securely to a support. Keep them well supplied with feed and moisture to build up a strong flowering framework. To encourage the development of side shoots, pinch out the growing point in July, otherwise this produces a premature flower which inhibits the growth of the side shoots that will carry the main display in late August.

In order to achieve show quality blooms, stopping, shoot thinning, and disbudding will be necessary; in this way all the plant's energies are concentrated into the production of a limited number of potentially perfect flowers.

After the frosts of autumn have blackened the dahlia foliage, all top growth is cut away and the tubers are lifted. Leave the roots in an airy shed to dry, a process which makes it easy to clean away all the soil which adhered to the roots when they were lifted. With an old pair of scissors I clip off the whisker-like roots which grow on the swollen tubers. The dahlia stems have a pithy central core, and to reduce the risk of this holding moisture to cause rotting, I push a piece of heavy-gauge wire through the middle of the stem. This clears out the pith to leave an air passage which thoroughly dries out the central root portion. In order to prevent a mix-up in the spring I tie a label to the stem with the name of the variety clearly printed on it.

8

Old Roses
(Shrubs and Climbers)

The rose is the most celebrated of all garden flowers. In one form or another, and for a variety of purposes roses have been cultivated for at least three thousand years. Throughout every period of recorded history there are references to roses. In festival and legend roses have figured as a token of passion, esteem, fidelity, triumph, and, on occasion, remembrance.

Like the stages of man, the rose has played in its time many parts. Roman brides and bridegrooms were crowned with wreaths of roses and verbena plucked by the bride herself, typifying love and purity. In more martial vein Persian warriors wore garlands of roses on their shields. The Persians believed also that the roses burst into bloom only when the nightingale sang. Rose petals were scattered in the path of conquering armies, and were used as decoration on the figureheads of warships. A wreath of roses worn around the head was in the more degenerate days of the Roman empire supposed to prevent intoxication. Yet the flower also figured frequently in burial ceremonies, particularly those of the Greeks and Romans, who decorated their tombs, as the inscription at Ravenna indicates, with 'The Queen of Flowers'.

Roses also played an important part in the pharmacopoeia as a constituent of herbal medicine, to strengthen the heart, stomach, and liver, to stop coughs, to prevent vomiting, and to cure lung diseases. A cosmetic in rose water, skin creams, and lotions, the flower has for centuries been used for skin care.

The rose has been studied by botanists, extolled by poets, cultivated and hybridised by gardeners. It has been an object of veneration, decoration, and utility, an associate of mirth and celebration, a companion of death and lamentation.

There are many fascinating fables accounting for the various colours of roses. Venus, trying to hide Adonis from the vengeance of Mars in a thicket of roses, pricked herself on a thorn, staining the white rose-red with her blood. Ayeshah, wife of Mohammed, suspected of infidelity with a Persian youth, was asked to dip a bunch of white roses in the fountain to prove her innocence. Should the flowers emerge unchanged, the accusation would be seen as a lie. They were plunged into the water where they turned yellow – which is, indeed, fortunate, for the same

Climbing roses at the
Bagatelle in Paris

rose is the parent of so many of our yellow bedding roses. Fact, legend, folklore are so inextricably intertwined that even research historians have not untangled the web sufficiently to reveal the whole story. The argument over which are the true species and which natural hybrids flares up at intervals.

Some facts do emerge. The birthplace of the rose as we know it was discovered to be Persia, but fossilised roses have been discovered in Europe, America, and Asia. The 'foundation' roses, well-known and widely grown throughout Europe in the sixteenth century, were *Rosa gallica*, *R. moschata*, *R. damascena*, and *R. alba*. These are generally supposed to have come from 'the land of the Saracens' – that is, the region of Arabic–Mohammedan influence in Syria and areas nearby. Persia's contribution to rose history came in the introduction of *R. foetida*

in the late nineteenth century, which brought a true yellow to European roses for the first time. However, the birthplace of the modern rose is surely China, as it was these introductions that brought in repeat flowering, or the remontant habit, so important in modern roses.

The profitable cultivation of roses as a commercial venture began in Persia about the year 1612 with the distillation of attar of roses, an industry which spread into Europe through Turkey. The largest centre of rose growing for perfumery was located in the valley of Struma in the Balkans where Damask roses were grown in large quantities to provide the material for processing. Even three hundred years ago growing roses for garden ornament was not widespread. There were possibly a few plants in monastery gardens, or in the large demesne. Not until the Empress Joséphine began to collect roses for her garden at Malmaison, France, early last century, in all over a hundred species and varieties, did rose growing become fashionable. Since then interest in roses, their cultivation and the breeding of new varieties has increased at a still accelerating speed. Specialist

Climbing roses floodlit at
La Roseraie de l'Haÿ les Roses, Paris

Rosa canina

societies were soon formed to cater for those who shared an enthusiasm for growing roses even more precise in formation and exquisite in colour.

The story of the rose in Britain is well documented. In 1629 Parkinson writes of 'a great variete of roses' which grew in his garden. Not counting the species, those amounted to only thirty sorts. I wonder what effect a modern list of roses would have on that learned gentleman!

In this country there are a number of wild species. The sap from the roots of *R. canina* is listed in herbals as a cure for rabies, which explains the popular name Dog rose and the botanical title. The Field rose, *R. arvensis*, smaller than the Dog rose, is quite common in southern and central England. The Burnet rose, *R. pimpinellifolia*, with creamy-white flowers and prickly stems, is found in coastal areas. Sweet briar, *R. eglanteria* or *R. rubiginosa*, is the least common, growing mainly on lime soils, and is distinguished by dark pink petals and more rounded leaflets which are sweetly fragrant. *R. villosa*, the Downy rose, is identified by double-toothed leaflets, pink flowers, and very large fruits which are distinctly ornamental, useful also for making preserves. The flowering times are more or less the same in all the native species, though there is not sufficient difference in growth or character of flower for cross-pollination to produce any wide variation in the resulting hybrids. *R. canina* has, however, been used extensively as a root-stock on which to bud Shrub, Hybrid tea, and Floribunda roses, as it will grow well in most soils, an adaptability which is of considerable importance.

In their wild state roses occur only in the northern hemisphere, and of the two hundred or so species only about one-tenth figure in the parentage of popular modern hybrids. Again, Gerard in his *Herbal* written in 1597 lists amongst others five roses which have made an important contribution: *R. gallica*, *R. damascena*, *R. centifolia*, *R. alba* and *R. moschata*.

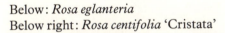

Below: *Rosa eglanteria*
Below right: *Rosa centifolia* 'Cristata'

Left: *Rosa damascena*

R. gallica, the French rose, being among the most ancient, is considered to be one of the earliest which produced semi-double and double flowers; these vary in colour from pink to dark red. The dwarf, compact habit and healthy, dark green foliage would undoubtedly be noted by early rosarians as desirable qualities in a garden plant. *R. gallica* is one parent of the hybrid China and Bourbon roses. It is the only true red-flowered species native to Europe. The red semi-double Apothecary's rose, *R. gallica officinalis*, is unusual in that the colour and scent of the flower is retained almost totally in the dried state. They were at one time widely used as a tonic tisane.

R. damascena, the Damask rose, forms a prickly bush up to 5 feet (1·5 m) high with white to red, very fragrant flowers opening in June and July. Apart from giving rise to the much-discussed 'York and Lancaster' rose, it is also one parent of the Hybrid Perpetuals which became popular in the nineteenth century.

R. centifolia, the Provence rose, is a fairly loose-habited shrub growing to 4 feet (1·2 m) or slightly more. The clear pink flowers appear late in June or July, and are frequently featured in Dutch flower paintings of the nineteenth century.

The White rose of York, *Rosa × alba semi-plena*, must be one of the earliest known hybrids, possibly between *R. dumetorum* and *R. gallica*. It is a spreading shrub up to 8 feet (2·4 m) high, with white flowers quite often shaded with pink, and grey-green leaves. One of the loveliest hybrids from *R. × alba*, which appeared in the late eighteenth century, is 'Céleste', a perfectly delightful shrub. The soft pink flowers against the grey-green leaves combine to present a picture which will grace any garden.

R. moschata is a vigorous, rampant climber, which I have seen growing 30 feet (9 m) along a retaining wall and, in the same garden, at least the same distance through and over an old tree. More than four hundred years have elapsed since it was introduced to gardeners in Britain from Italian gardens. The flowers, which open in August continuing until the frosts, are single white and intensely fragrant. The true *R. moschata* of garden

Below: *Rosa* 'Céleste'

Far left: *Rosa gallica officinalis*
Left: *Rosa gallica versicolor*
Right: *Rosa moschata*

tradition is rare possibly because it is tender and needs a sheltered corner. Also, the late flowering habit would not now be considered an advantage when ever-blooming climbers are available which flower five months of the year and take up less space. Nevertheless, *R. moschata* could at least lay claim to being the first climbing rose to be grown in British gardens, and even more important, through the China roses is an ancestor of the modern HT, the Hybrid Musk, and some of the popular ramblers. Indeed, it is surprising just how many modern roses originate in the distant past from one of the five roses listed by Gerard.

Fresh impetus and interest was injected into rose hybridisation and growing by the introductions from China of roses which were repeat, or, as they are termed, 'perpetual blooming', a character not evident in the species cultivated in this country or Europe. There were four original China roses introduced to European gardens about 1790, but two – 'Slater's Crimson', and, more important, 'Parson's Pink' because it was hardier – arrived first to be adopted very quickly by nurserymen. 'Parson's Pink' crossed with the already established musk roses produced the Noisette roses, which are repeat flowering. They are best pruned during the winter, when weak shoots and worn-out branches should be taken out.

'Gloire de Dijon' was one of the early Noisette with well-formed flowers, buff-yellow tinted pink, in evidence from June to September. This hybrid flowers with reasonable freedom when grown on a north wall, and is still a widely acclaimed variety.

'Aimée Vibert' is even older, with white flowers which look best if the 15-foot (4·5-m) shoots are allowed to arch out naturally on a bank or over a retaining wall.

The marriage between the China roses and Damask produced the Bourbon group, which originate from the Ile de Bourbon. It is a mixed group characterised by vigorous growth, rather lax habit, and globular blooms. Most splendid of these is

Top left: *Rosa* 'Gloire de Dijon'
Top right: *Rosa* 'Parson's Pink'
Above: *Rosa* 'Mme Isaac Pereire'

Opposite
Top: *Rosa moyesii*
Centre: *Rosa xanthina* 'Canary Bird'
Below: *Rosa* 'Frau Karl Druschki'

the 'Zéphirine Drouhin' which, though introduced in 1868, still retains a unique place in gardens. The stems are thornless, the young foliage copper, flushed purple. Vivid cerise-pink flowers, delightfully scented, open in continuous succession from June to Christmas given freedom from frost. 'Zéphirine Drouhin' alone assures the Bourbon rose of a proud place in the record books. Another of the truly worthwhile Bourbon hybrids is 'Mme Isaac Pereire', which grows into a large bush. The flowers are large and cup-shaped; the deep pink petals, rolled at the tips, are very fragrant.

Almost as the first crosses using the Chinese introductions were being made came two more roses from China. The first was bought from a Cantonese nursery – 'Hume's Blush', described as a Tea-scented China. The second, 'Park's Yellow Tea-scented China', also Cantonese, arrived a few years later. For the rose breeder it added a new colour to be used in cross-pollination. The fragrance was unlike that of the established varieties. 'Used' is possibly the wrong word to describe early attempts at cross-pollination. Growers left things very much to nature, planting groups of selected bushes near to each other for the bees to work on. Only in the late 1800s did the hybridiser start selective pollination by hand, a process which enabled exact details of parentage to be kept.

Once begun, new species of roses were continually being introduced and entered for use into the rose breeders' stud books. Two are individual and exceptional garden plants. *R. moyesii* commemorates the Reverend Moyes. Introduced in 1903, the tall, upright bush with fern-like foliage and single flowers of dusky crimson is a noble sight. In autumn, when large flask-shaped hips show vivid red against the yellowing leaves, the bush is once more superb. I have grown several dozen *R. moyesii* from seed over the years; all have been good, although several were outstanding, with large, dusky-red blooms the colour of bonfire embers on a frosty night. The other, from Korea, is *R. xanthina*, of which the form 'Canary Bird' is the best known. The canary-yellow flowers which cover the long arching branches in May to June are borne in such profusion that the bush becomes a fountain of gold.

The influence of the Chinese roses was given fresh impetus when the rather tender, yellow-flowered climber, *R. gigantea*, was discovered and the possibility realised of raising climbing roses with yellow flowers. So the raising of more new garden roses progressed from the casual, open pollination of pre-1870 to the hand-selected, and finally to the line-breeding, tissue culture of the present day.

Certain roses grow best on a particular type of soil. Burnet roses, as would be expected, succeed on a light soil. Most of these will grow in well-maintained garden soil and a place in the sun.

Hybrid Perpetuals are a mixture of so many groups, starting with Bourbon roses, that tracing the family tree is extremely difficult. Best-known of the Hybrid Perpetuals is 'Frau Karl Druschki', the loveliest of white roses but unfortunately without scent. Growth is vigorous, up to 5 feet (1·5 m) with well-formed

white flowers opening in succession over many months. 'Hugh Dickson', another HP, was for a long time the best red rose for growing on a wall or fence. The height is around 9 feet (2·7 m), and the rich crimson, sweetly scented flowers are a good shape. Up to six years ago there was a plant of 'Hugh Dickson' growing on the wall of a house in Yorkshire which to my knowledge was forty years old, still treasured for its beauty and long-flowering season. It should be pruned in winter, taking out weak and worn-out growth; long, young growth is then tipped back to ripe wood.

Hybrid Musks are a mixture of so many breeding lines, Multiflora, Noisette, and Hybrid tea, which have produced a race of recurrent-flowering, strong-growing shrubs. Pruning consists of removing dead flower trusses, and then removing weak, diseased, or worn-out shoots in winter to encourage young shoots. I once designed a double border planted with shrub

Above: Climbing rose 'American Pillar' framing the lovely avenues of La Roseraie de l'Haÿ les Roses

Right: *Rosa* 'Hugh Dickson'
Far right: *Rosa rugosa* 'Rubra'

roses, including Hybrid Musks, which in June was such an interplay of muted colour tones and fragrance that years later I still remember it with intense pleasure.

'Buff Beauty', with well-formed blooms of apricot-yellow, was well represented because cuttings rooted so easily. 'Cornelia' flowered continuously from mid-June onwards, a deep bronze-apricot in bud, opening to buff-pink. 'Moonlight', a *R. moschata* hybrid with the other parent unknown, is another 'Musk rose' of merit. The huge flower trusses, carried on young shoots which follow the first flush of bloom, are typically musk-scented.

The species *R. rugosa* is a native of northern China, Korea, and Japan, where it grows wild in sandy soils near the coast. Yet in complete contradiction to what I could have expected, both budded stock and plants grown from cuttings grew well in a Yorkshire garden where the soil is a heavy clay. Though *R. rugosa* has been cultivated for centuries in China, it did not make a positive influence on European gardens until the late nineteenth century. Breeders then appeared to note the hardiness, disease resistance and flower colour. *R. rugosa* cross-pollinates so readily with other roses that it is not surprising there are so many varieties of this shrub on offer. All old, spent stems and twig-like, non-productive growth should be removed during winter.

Within the *R. rugosa* species, the form 'Rubra' is a magnificent shrub where space can be afforded, the deep crimson flowers relieved by cream-coloured stamens. In autumn the leaves colour pale yellow and show the dark red hips to advantage. Also showing definite *rugosa* characteristics, 'Roseraie de l'Haÿ' has what could be described as a luxuriously coloured, velvet-textured flower. The crimson-purple petals are delightful seen with sunlight shining through them. The plant is lovely in association with Regal lilies, whose white flowers contrast with the regal purple-crimson of the rose. Of so many so-called 'rugosa' hybrids it can be said that the relationship is hard to identify, but not so with 'Sarah Van Fleet', which in dark green foliage and upright growth mirrors its ancestry. The freely produced flowers are pink, semi-double, and sweetly scented.

Breeding continues, and each year new Hybrid shrub roses are released on to the market. Most have the perpetual flowering habit, but in many cases they lack that impossible-to-define specific called 'character'. 'Fritz Nobis' with *R. rubiginosa* as the seed parent is, amongst the newcomers, good value. The HT-shaped flowers are pink with darker shading, and the lovely clove scent is retained. 'Nevada' is said to have the excellent *R. moyesii* as one parent. A large bush, its branches 7 feet (2 m) long arch over to display a mass of creamy-white flowers, each measuring 4 to 5 inches (10 to 13 cm) across, making a garden pageant of extravagant beauty. As with nearly all roses, both species and hybrids, semi-hard or hardwood cuttings root very easily.

That most excellent rose 'Queen Elizabeth' is too tall for inclusion with the Floribunda bedding roses. Growing to a height of 6 feet (1·8 m), it gives the best display when grown as a hedge or grouped in a shrub border. Silver-pink, HT-shaped flowers open in clusters for four or five months from late June.

Climbing and Rambling roses contribute so much to the beauty of gardens, covering house walls, fences, and unsightly buildings with a living screen of magnificent flowers. There are so many to choose from in the various groups: strong-growing 'Kiftsgate' and 'Wedding Day', which are too large for any but the very big garden, to the ramblers like 'Violette', with clusters of flowers of such a dark purple that they would be lost shadows were it not for the contrasting yellow stamens.

R. sempervirens, *R. wichuriana*, and *R. multiflora* all contribute blood or bone to their virtue. I can only select those which have served me well. For the sixty-two years since being introduced 'Albertine' has carved a special niche in gardeners'

Rosa 'Kew Rambler'

Above: *Rosa* 'Nevada'
Right: *Rosa* 'New Dawn'

affections. Though there is only one display of flowers, in midsummer, the dark green leaves vanish under a mound of multi-toned salmon on pink on buff flowers. Both as a Climber and as a free-growing shrub this is a rose to grow fond of; the colour and fragrance make it one of the choice *wichuriana* Ramblers.

'Félicité et Perpétue' is an old, bone-hardy Rambler to which I owe a debt of gratitude. For six years it disguised one of the ugliest buildings ever to pollute a garden. The foliage is practically perennial, the flowers are pink in bud opening to white – millions of crimp-petalled pompons. The fragrance is delicately positive without being intrusive. 'Kew Rambler' deserves to be better known, having been introduced seventy years ago, and earned an Award of Merit sixty years ago. The specimen in my charge clothed an interlap wooden screen 25 feet (7·6 m) long with masking greenery; in June the flowers were dark pink with a white eye, until, as October came, masses of small orange hips appeared. 'Mermaid', the result of a cross between *R. bracteata* and a Tea rose, is tender and best grown on a sheltered wall. There it will open a succession of single yellow blooms 4 inches (10 cm) wide from June to October. Pruning should be restricted to removing dead or damaged branches.

'New Dawn' is one of those roses that are guaranteed to grow and flower anywhere and to please, if not to earn unqualified adoration. It is a good rose for general planting, and has silver-pink, scented flowers perpetually during the summer. No one who has seen the Rambler 'Wedding Day' growing into the apple tree then trailing over the path in the East Lambrooke Manor garden in June – a white-petalled, orange-scented curtain – will forget this exquisite picture. It is vigorous indeed, but a Rambler which can be left very much to its own devices once established.

The so-called 'Old-fashioned' roses would not have survived in competition with so many modern introductions if they were not such interesting and lovely plants. Old roses are more perennial in character than the HT and Floribunda bedding-rose varieties, important though these two groups may be.

9
Modern Roses
(Hybrid tea and Floribunda)

The modern bedding rose is entirely a product of the plant breeder's art. With one root of the family tree in China, the other in Europe, man was the marriage broker who brought the widely separate cultures together; for, while the European gardeners were busily raising new varieties from crosses between *Rosa gallica, R. moschata, R. phoenicea, R. damascena*, and others, so the Chinese with an even larger number of species to work with were themselves developing entirely separate groups of hybrids. All these roses, European and Chinese – or, more correctly, Western and Eastern Asian – though variable in themselves offered only a limited programme to the plant breeders. The bringing together of the separate cultures broadened the scope and possibility of variation to an almost unlimited extent. In the latter half of the eighteenth century *R. chinensis* arrived in Europe and in due course worked a transformation in the habit of growth and flowering period of our garden roses.

The modern, dwarf-growing, repeat-flowering Hybrid tea rose is infinitely more valuable as a garden decoration than the Shrub rose, which flowers only once a year. Characteristically, the flower has a definite, pointed bud. This opens to show many velvet-like petals, all of which, in a good show rose, will be reflexed and arranged perfectly to provide the central cone. Curiously, in the wild state *R. chinensis* – soon dubbed the 'China rose' – is often a climber 20 feet (6 m) high. The repeat-flowering form is a bush only 4 feet (1·2 m) high, known in Chinese gardens, according to historians, since the sixteenth century. Then early in the nineteenth century came *R. gigantea*, the Chinese rose which established the habit of continuous flowering, not just in the Hybrid tea roses but in many of the Shrub roses also, notably the Hybrid Musks and Perpetuals. Some dictionaries still list this most noteworthy rose under *R. odorata*, while the latest edition of Bean places it under *R. gigantea*. Piece by piece the essential parts of the genealogical jigsaw link together. *R. chinensis* contributed the repeat-flowering character, while *R. gigantea* added the high, pointed shape and characteristic scent to the individual blooms. In European gardens *R. gigantea* proved tender, flourishing outdoors only in the milder parts of the country, a quality inherent in its tea-rose

A colourful bed of Floribunda roses at Parc de la Tête d'Or, Lyon

progeny. But from China came the famous ancestral roses, popularly known as the 'stud' roses: 'Parson's Pink, 'Hume's Blush Tea-Scented China', and others, including 'Slater's Crimson', which is thought to be the parent of the 'Portland Rose'. To simplify a rather complex genealogical tree a cross between one of the Damask roses with a hybrid China rose resulted in the Hybrid Perpetuals, which, from 1825, held a proud place in gardens. Unlike the tea roses, Hybrid Perpetuals are quite hardy and need no protection, whether grown as dwarf bush or climber. Hundreds of varieties were raised, but the first Hybrid Perpetual is generally agreed to have been 'Rose du Roi'.

Obviously, nurserymen and gardeners being of an enquiring mind made the cross between the tender tea rose with well-shaped, scented flowers and the hardy perpetuals – and the result was Hybrid tea. Fortunately, the cross which produced the first named HT rose, 'La France', is believed to have been between the Hybrid Perpetual, 'Mme Victor Verdier' and the tea rose 'Mme Bravy'. I grew 'La France' in my last garden, and can imagine how enthusiastically the large, double, silver-pink flowers with their lovely scent would be received by rose-growing devotees. Unlike many HTs, 'La France' is better grown on a light soil.

There is no mystery now about how new roses are raised. Without going into details about genetics, very simply, roses possess in the same flower both stamens (male organs) and pistil (female organ). For fertilisation to take place and seeds to ripen for sowing, pollen has to be transferred from stamens to that part of the pistil called the stigma. There the pollen grain germinates, grows down, and fertilises the ovules. Once fertilisation is accomplished the ovules swell and ripen to become fertile seeds. A species – for example, *R. gigantea* – pollinated with pollen from another rose of the same species, will offer seed which when sown gives rise to plants in most cases identical with the parents. What the hybridiser is trying to do is to breed new varieties with large, more perfectly formed, fragrant flowers, and foliage which is resistant to attack by fungus disease. Therefore different species or varieties are crossed, so that by a different genetic combination the best qualities of both parents are united in the offspring. No two of the resulting seedlings will be identical. Possibly out of

'Comte de Chambord',
a 'Portland Rose'

Rosa 'La France'

Rosa foetida 'Persiana'

Rosa 'Soleil d'Or'

hundreds of seedlings grown only one or two will prove to have any of the desired qualities. Even the expert hybridist with a sound knowledge of genetics, a well-equipped laboratory, and years of experience can shorten the odds against producing one good rose out of thousands only by a very small amount. The amateur who casually cross-pollinates two favourite roses could produce a magnificent new variety.

For those who wish to try their hand with hybridisation this is my own method. Select the parents. I choose the pollen parent (or male) for colour, the seed parent (female) for vigour and flower shape. To prevent the female parent being fertilised by its own pollen, all the stamens have to be removed with a pair of eyebrow tweezers. The emasculated flower is then sealed inside a muslin or paper bag so that neither insects nor wind can bring pollen from elsewhere. When the stigma is sticky (receptive), pollen from the chosen male parent is dusted on to it. The protective covering is replaced afterwards. When there are obvious signs – the stigma withers, the seed pod swells – that the cross has taken, remove the cover. When the seed pod (hip) is red-ripe and soft to the touch, extract the seeds and sow them immediately. Some will germinate the following spring, some may not show signs of growth for twelve months. Pot the seedlings off, then let them grow for one season before lining them out in nursery rows. There is an excitement, a sense of anticipation, in watching rose seedlings come up to flower, which grows more compelling with each new batch of seedlings raised. That I have never produced a top quality HT in no way lessens the pleasure that growing roses from seed has given me.

Once the initial cross tea rose on to perpetual had been effected it could be repeated *ad infinitum*. The resulting HT offspring could in due course be crossed with each other, or back-crossed to the China tea or Hybrid Perpetual.

Even then the story is not complete. Because of the constant demand for newer, improved varieties on the part of an increasingly aware gardening public, a cross was made between the yellow Persian rose, *R. foetida* 'Persiana', and the Hybrid Perpetual 'Antoine Ducher', producing a seedling of little merit except hybrid vigour. When this seedling flowered, the seed capsule ripened and a self-sown seedling which grew alongside the parent bush developed orange-yellow, double blooms. This was named 'Soleil d'Or'. From this yellow rose came a new brilliantly coloured race of HT roses in yellow and orange. This giant step forward in rose breeding was due entirely to the untiring efforts of Pernet-Duchet. Thus one successful cross-pollination can introduce a seedling which influences plant breeding in a most dramatic way. Hybridisers went on to extend the strain of Pernetiana roses (as they were called) into an ever-richer variety of colours which until 'Soleil d'Or' had seemed impossible. 'Mme Edouard Herriot', one of the best-known Pernetiana, is an example: the petals are a bright terracotta, fading to rose-pink. I remember being given the task of spraying this particular rose against black spot during my training; unfortunately, the leaves are very prone to this disease.

In 1870 there occurred another one of those happy accidents which mark significant milestones in rose history. In a nursery near Lyon, amongst a batch of seedling *R. multiflora* roses of Japanese origin, a M. Guillot noticed a white form, which he called 'Paquèrette'. The accidental pollen exchange was thought to have been between multiflora and dwarf pink China or Fairy Rose. Seed harvested from the white-flowered 'Paquerette' grew on to give two dwarf seedlings with pompon flower heads, the first Polyantha. From such a modest, inauspicious beginning came an entirely new race of roses to compete with the HT for pride of place in our gardens. It is even more extraordinary that out of this second generation only two of the seedlings were shrubs and continuous-flowering; the remainder were once-flowering dwarf climbers. No doubt, the crosses between the Polypon or Polyantha and HT which produced 'Cecile Brunner' were made soon after. Even a hundred years after this is a most desirable, perfectly formed pale-pink, shaded-yellow Miniature rose. 'Perle d'Or', even more exquisite, appeared four years later. Dwarf in habit, the perfectly shaped buds open pale orange-pink and are very fragrant.

Notable though these two early hybrid Polyantha roses may be, it was a rose breeder in Denmark who took the rose world by assault when in 1924 he introduced a distinct group of roses. The Poulsen roses (as they came to be called) were achieved by crossing Polypon (Polyantha) onto Hybrid tea. Svend Poulsen took pollen from the HT 'Red Star' to fertilise the Polypom 'Orleans'. From this union two seedlings emerged, one, with semi-double, medium-sized bright rose-pink flowers on strong upstanding stems, was duly named 'Else Poulsen'. The other, though equally vigorous, had bright, cherry-red single flowers and was called 'Kirsten Poulsen'. The garden in which I worked as a youth had a hedge of 'Kirsten Poulsen' to divide the rose garden. The strong, upright growth is ideally suited to the purpose. Other Poulsen varieties followed, 'Karen Poulsen' and 'Poulsen's Pink' being the best known. The name that was

A lovely combination of Floribunda roses and a Standard rose in a public park

Above and right: *Rosa* 'The Fairy'

Floribundas
Left: *Rosa* 'Mountbatten'
Top: *Rosa* 'Iceberg'
Above: *Rosa* 'Evelyn Fison'

originally given to the new race of roses, Hybrid Polyantha, has subsequently been changed to 'Floribunda'. These do not possess the size of individual blooms when compared to their rival, the Hybrid Tea rose. Here the flowers are less pointed in shape and are borne in large trusses continually throughout the rose season.

Of all the bedding roses, HT, Polyantha (or Floribunda), no single variety has achieved greater popularity than 'Peace'. Raised by F. Meilland in France, the breeding line includes some illustrious roses, 'George Dickson' and 'Margaret McGredy' being two well known in this country. The seedling 'Peace' flowered in 1935, stocks were budded in 1936 and blossomed the same autumn. What must have been the feeling of M. Meilland on seeing the first flower fully open! Large, full-bodied, each yellow petal edged with pink, and the shape exceptional. Add to these the qualities of vigorous constitution, glossy, disease-resistant foliage, and virtually weather-proof flowers. What a proud justification for a lifetime's work! In my experience 'Peace' should be only lightly pruned or growth is made at the expense of flowers.

Climbing 'sports' of HT roses do occur; even the re-doubtable 'Peace' has a climbing offspring which, unfortunately, is shy of flower. Why some HT produce climbing branches is, no doubt, explained by the presence of a Climber rose, *R. chinensis*,

Floribundas
Top: *Rosa* 'Anne Cocker'
Above: *Rosa* 'Anne Harkness'
Right: *Rosa* 'Picasso'

in their ancestry. Occasionally the mutation which brought forth a dwarf repeat-flowering shrub reverts to type, and we get a climbing HT – which proves yet again what a splendidly accommodating plant the rose is!

In the majority of cases roses are propagated by budding. This consists of taking a plump, dormant bud from a healthy shoot, and then grafting it on to suitable root-stock, usually in July and August. Root-stocks can be bought by an amateur grower who is keen to raise new roses for home use. The stocks used are *canina* or selections from it, *laxa, multiflora*, and, for standard roses, *rugosa* is still popular. The stocks, which preferably should be the thickness of the little finger or a drawing pencil, are lined out 4 to 6 inches (10 to 15 cm) apart the previous autumn or winter.

Take the buds from the middle of a healthy branch which has just flowered. Cut the whole branch and strip off the leaves, except for an inch of stalk under each bud, which is left as a handle. The thorns are also removed. Holding the branch firmly, take a sharp budding knife, make a cut half an inch (1·2 cm) below the selected bud. Then, half an inch above the bud insert the knife at a right angle to the stem and draw it down under the first cut. The piece of bark with bud attached can be lifted clear. Always handle it by the leaf stalk, for on no account must the piece of bark known as the shield be allowed to get dirty.

Clean the soil away from the base of the selected stock; wipe it if necessary with a soft cloth. Make a horizontal cut at the neck of the stock, then a vertical cut from near the root up to meet it. The two cuts form a letter T. Gently lift the edges of the bark, insert the shield and fix it firmly in place with raffia, rubber, or plastic ties.

Roses can, of course, be grown from seed, but only species will breed true; hybrid seed will produce a rare old mixture – most of them useless.

Most roses can be propagated from cuttings taken in September to October from well-ripened shoots of the current year's growth. Cuttings should be about 8 inches (20 cm) long or more – up to 15 inches (38 cm) in some cases. Remove all the leaves from the bottom third of the cutting, then after dipping the base in rooting powder dibble them into a sandy compost soil or cutting mixture made up of 2 parts soil, 2 parts sharp sand, 1 part peat. The following autumn all cuttings which have rooted can be transplanted to flowering quarters.

Propagation by layering is the method used to increase stocks of Rambler roses, particularly the *wichuriana* hybrids. Indeed, this is the easiest way, for quite often shoots which touch the soil will root naturally with no help from the gardener. Select a shoot of the previous year's growth, twist or wound a section which can be conveniently pegged down to the ground to stimulate rooting, then bury the treated section in a sandy compost. A heavy stone or peg is essential to hold the layer firmly in place. The following

Right (all Hybrid Tea):
Rosa 'Peace'
Rosa 'Pink Favourite'
Rosa 'Whisky Mac'
Rosa 'Alec's Red'

Far right:
Floribunda roses make a good foil for yucca in full flower at Parc de la Tête d'Or, Lyon

Rosa 'Silver Jubilee' (Hybrid Tea)

autumn the layers will be rooted well enough for lifting. This method is not suitable for climbing HT or Floribunda roses, which are better budded on vigorous root-stock.

Roses are cursed with the reputation that they will grow anywhere. This quite often means they are rammed in with no thought given to their cultural requirements. That they grow and flower is a tribute to their resilience, though compared with roses grown in well-prepared soil and properly cared for they are mere shadows of their real selves. Roses should be planted in full sun, away from trees, whose roots compete with them for nutriment. There is also less risk of disease if the site is open with free air circulation.

Shrub roses make admirable feature plants in the ornamental border. Bedding roses, the HT, and Floribunda look very attractive against the green background of a lawn.

Roses thrive in a heavy soil so long as it is well drained and cultivated. However, all soils whatever their composition, will grow roses if plenty of farm manure, compost, or similar material is worked in two or three months before the date set for planting. The finest roses I ever grew were planted in what were previously grass fields, which gives some indication of the soil condition they enjoy.

Arguments about whether autumn or spring planting is best are never resolved. After growing many thousand roses, autumn is the time I choose, providing the soil is in good condition. Quite often the nurseries lift the bushes early in the autumn, so they

might as well be in my care as in theirs. Also the rose sends out new roots in midwinter – late January to February – so they establish much more quickly than if the planting were delayed until spring. Any bushes planted later than March should be puddled in – have their roots dipped in what is virtually liquid mud as a precaution against their drying out. Before planting, whatever the season, I shorten back the roots with a pair of secateurs or a sharp knife. This stimulates the growth of fine feeding roots.

Dig a hole large and deep enough to accommodate the roots comfortably, spread the fibres out horizontally, then work in about 4 inches (10 cm) of soil amongst the roots. Firm this down with your feet, then complete the filling in with soil from the bed. The junction between the root and stem (budding point) should then be about 1 inch (2·5 cm) below the soil surface.

I prefer to prune established roses in early March. First cut

An attractive corner
at the Bagatelle, Paris

away all dead, weak, or damaged branches, then prune all the really strong branches back to about six buds, the rest back to three buds. There can be no set rules: the severity or otherwise of pruning depends very much on the variety. Hard pruning of a strong-growing variety like 'Peace' brings more wood and no flowers. Floribunda–Polyantha are not pruned quite so hard. Again, I first clean out all moribund or unwanted branches, then cut back the remainder to seven or eight buds.

Climbing roses should be pruned in their formative years to build up a permanent framework of branches. Short growths which spring from framework branches I cut back to three buds. Strong young shoots are trained in to replace any of the original framework as required.

To get a continuous display of flowers from June to autumn, all roses need to be fed: 2 oz (57 g) of balanced fertiliser to the square yard (0·8 m) in mid-April, plus a mulch of rotted manure, peat, compost or whatever is available in early May. Then in early July a further 2 oz (57 g) of fertiliser per square yard will keep the roses in flower. They also require a constant supply of moisture throughout the growing season. A mulch of organic matter put on the soil will help, but during dry weather watering with either a sprinkler or hosepipe so as to thoroughly saturate the soil will be of great benefit to the plants.

Suckers are shoots which grow from the root-stock and should be removed. Carefully trace the sucker shoot to its point of origin and then pull, NOT cut it away. Suckers are a result of incorrect planting or digging amongst established roses which has damaged the roots.

Pests and disease will attack even the well-maintained rose garden. There are on the market five or six products available to combat any disease or pest which has the temerity to attack our roses. Most important, correctly identify the pest or disease; then take steps to control it. Fungicides and pesticides used on the 'blanket' principle to control every scourge that could infest the garden can be dangerous. It is far better to know the culprit, and use a chemical which deals specifically with it – obeying the manufacturer's instructions exactly.

Below: *Rosa* 'Just Joey' (Hybrid Tea)

In a rose garden where the plants are pruned, fed, and watered correctly, I have always found two or three sprays to be enough. A three-tier programme would be a systemic insecticide in mid-May to control the first aphis (green-fly) infestation; in mid- to late-June a combined systemic insecticide and fungicide (green-fly and mildew control); in later August it may be necessary to repeat the fungal spray.

Fortunately, roses are the easiest of plants to grow, providing there is no lack of that most excellent fertiliser, common sense. Over the hundreds of years that they have been grown and admired they have earned a unique place in garden history and legend. The story has not yet been fully unfolded, and there are still species which have not been used by the hybridiser. Who knows what colours may evolve next year, perhaps a rose the colour of a Gentian or Delphinium? With roses no dream is impossible.

10
Chrysanthemums

Chrysos, 'golden' *anthos*, 'flower' – such is its meaning, though the word 'chrysanthemum' conjures up a picture in the mind's eye of mist-shrouded autumn days. The flower, by comparison with long-established favourites like the rose, is a newcomer. In 1789 a M. Blancard introduced three chrysanthemums from the Far East into Marseilles. Only one, 'Old Purple', survived, and stock eventually found its way to England. The story of the chrysanthemum in England began in 1796 with the 327th plate of the *Botanical Magazine*, which showed a plant which grew in Mr Colville's Nursery in King's Road, Chelsea. Between 1820 and 1830 upwards of forty varieties, either by means of seed or plants, were imported, and the foundations were laid of what is now a considerable industry. Once the hybridisers had succeeded in setting and ripening seed on plants grown in this country, the production of new varieties could begin in earnest.

The so-called 'Autumn' chrysanthemums are descendants of the white-flowered Chinese *Chrysanthemum morifolium* (*sinensis*), or yellow-flowered *C. indicum* species. In 1846 Robert Fortune, a plant hunter and explorer extraordinary, sent home to England roots of the Chusan daisy, which was to be the parent of a whole new race, the very popular Pompon varieties.

Though of the same family as the daisy which stars so many of our lawns with white, it is only in the wild species that the chrysanthemum shows a marked resemblance to our modest British weed. Both *C. morifolium* (*sinensis*) and *C. indicum* show a yellow disc surrounded by ray florets. By selection the fertile central disc florets have been replaced by the more brightly coloured female ray petals. Double flowers are more sought after for garden decoration and floristry than the wild singles. Indeed, it is uncommon, for obvious reasons, to find full double forms of any plants in the wild, for if the bisexual disc florets have become unisexual female florets, the plant cannot set seed to reproduce itself. Full doubles are only preserved in our gardens by vegetative propagation. They are a product of the hybridiser's art, and are perpetuated by the gardener's skill. Even when giving the appearance of being full double, quite often the chrysanthemum preserves sufficient of the disc florets to produce seed which is of value in hybridisation.

Chrysanthemum 'Bonny Blush'

Much of the work of hybridising had already been done before the flower reached Europe. Since then, the process of selection and improvement on an established foundation has continued to give an ever-increasing range of hybrids, collectively known as *Chrysanthemum* × *hortorum*.

Before dealing with the intricacies of the classification of *C.* × *hortorum* and its cultivation under garden conditions, it will be helpful to describe the other species which, though not so widely grown, are useful garden plants. Four chrysanthemums are

native to this country: Corn marigold, *C. segetum*; Ox-eye daisy, *C. leucanthemum*; Feverfew, *C. parthenium*; and the debatable *C. vulgare*, the Common tansy, which is more often listed as *Tanacetum*. All flower in the summer time. Feverfew, which is often in abundance in or around gardens, is recommended in herbals as a treatment for migraine. Certainly, anyone who can relish the strong-tasting leaves deserves to be cured. Migraine sufferers have assured me it is effective.

In all there are over a hundred species widely distributed throughout the world. *C. alpinum*, a good garden plant, is easily raised from seed. The annual species are colourful plants and are usually sown direct into the open where they are to flower. Most of the perennial species are well suited by conditions in the herbaceous or mixed border, providing that the soil is well drained. Some species are valuable as a source of pyrethrum powder, a well-known insecticide still used in gardens, particularly as a control for white-fly.

C. carinatum is usually listed in seed catalogues as *C. tricolor* in the section devoted to hardy annuals. They are excellent value, whether grown for cut flowers or garden display. Seeds are sown in well-prepared soil in late April into shallow drills 12 inches (30 cm) apart, then thinned out after germination to a final spacing of 18 inches (46 cm) apart in the rows. The varieties on offer are often banded or zoned in contrasting colours. Stronger-growing *C. × spectabile* varieties, which are much in demand as cut flowers, grow up to 36 inches (91 cm) in height, and so need more space.

C. cinerariifolium is the source of pyrethrum insecticides, and is not widely grown in gardens. *C. coccineum*, parent of the extremely popular pyrethrum, was introduced from the Caucasus in 1807. Most of the varieties will thrive if given an open, fertile soil, fully exposed to all the available sunshine. Contrary to my experience with many herbaceous perennials, pyrethrums are best lifted and divided in late July, though early spring will do as second best. There are some delightful colour forms available, some double or semi-double, though I much prefer single-flowered sorts. The safest plan when selecting varieties is to visit a nursery offering stock and see the plants in flower, so avoiding disappointment. One word of warning: I never succeeded in growing pyrethrum in a heavy clay soil; the best results always came from those plants accommodated in medium to light loam.

A most reliable annual species can be found in *C. coronarium* from the Mediterranean region. It is about 3 to 4 feet (0·9 to 1·9 m) high with wide-branching stems bearing pale green leaves and cream or yellow flowers. The *C. nanum compactum* and *C. spathulatum* are selected forms of neater growth and more varied colours. They are very useful for direct sowing to fill gaps in the shrub or herbaceous border, and will continue in flower right through into the autumn.

As would be expected of a plant from the Canary Islands, Marguerite or Paris daisy, *C. frutescens*, is not reliably hardy. Overwintered in a frost-free greenhouse, then planted out with the summer bedding, it remains in bloom throughout the summer. A shrubby, dome-shaped bush 3 feet (0·9 m) high, covered in yellow-centred daisy flowers appeals to most tastes when surrounded by blue- or red-flowered bedding plants. The Paris daisy is available in shades of white, pink, or yellow, also with a choice of double flowers.

There are few more robust perennials than the Shasta daisy, *C. maximum*. The large white flowers of 'Esther Read', 'Wirral Supreme', and 'Bishopstone' have featured in borders down my

Chrysanthemum maximum 'Wirral Supreme'

Chrysanthemum parthenium

gardening years. They are most effective in herbaceous borders along with other popular perennials or (my preference) planted amongst Shrub roses where they act as a foil to the red-purple of 'Gypsy Boy', or 'Chiante'. Though happy in light soils, the strongest plants I looked after were rooted in a strong-bodied but well-drained clay. Division offers a ready means of increase when new stock is needed.

Though possessed of medical virtue Feverfew, *C. parthenium*, is best known as a dwarf edging to summer bedding. As with many native plants, 'Feverfew' takes so kindly to cultivation that it can become a nuisance. Confusingly, in seed catalogues this species is often listed under *Matricaria eximia*. Seed sown in late March will give well-grown plants for bedding out in late May. 'Golden Ball' and 'Snow Puff' will make good foils to the more violently aggressive bedding plants. The rounded hummocks of strongly scented leaves, which seldom grow more

Chrysanthemum 'Imp'
(Hardy Perennial)

Top and above:
Chrysanthemum 'Bunty' at
Bressingham Gardens, Norfolk

than 12 inches (30 cm) high are covered throughout the summer in full double button, mini chrysanthemum flowers. Legend has it that early botanists named the species *C. parthenium* because it saved the life of a workman who became giddy and fell from one of the walls while building the Parthenon. Such thoughts are the very romance of gardening.

Certainly, *C. uliginosum* is the most vigorously invasive of all the family that I have grown. Root-like underground stems push out from the parent to colonise new land far in excess of any space the beauty of the flowers deserves. Stalks 4 feet (1·2 m) high display sprays of white Dog daisy flowers in September.

Undoubtedly, it is the hybrid *C. × hortorum* which has made the biggest impact on the private garden and the horticultural industry. Reflecting on the origins of the extravagantly shaped, highly coloured varieties which grace gardens and greenhouses today, I could not help wondering what the thoughts of the man who made that first cross between *C. morifolium* (*sinensis*) and *C. indicum* were. Did he, three thousand years ago, understand the reasons for cross-pollination and carry out the operation as a deliberate attempt to produce a new race of plants, or was it an insect-aided accident? I doubt if any other single act of hybridisation in plants will ever equal that of the unknown Chinese gardener before gardens existed in Europe. What is certain is that chrysanthemums were grown in large quantities throughout China and Japan five hundred years before the birth of Christ.

Beginning with the Chinese hybrids with incurved florets, continuing on to the reflexing, shaggy-flowered Japanese types, mix in the Pompon-flowered Chusan chrysanthemum, let them all cross-hybridise, and the result is a modern florist's chrysanthemum in an almost infinite variety of shapes and almost every colour except blue. Specialist societies are not only an inevitable result, they become an absolute essential to bring order out of the chaos caused by a proliferation of new varieties.

The method of classification is based on the shape of the bloom, whether single or double, on how the florets are developed, and their shape and distribution on the central disc. Unfortunately, the majority of the varieties on offer, especially the large-flowered forms, do not make trouble-free hardy perennials. From the cutting stage to flowering they need a routine of staking, disbudding, and feeding which few other of our garden flowers demand. The end product is full justification for all the devoted care, a specialist would argue – a flower whose colour and shape epitomise the summit of perfection.

There are hardy or nearly hardy varieties, some which would be termed old-fashioned by a specialist grower. All will do well in fertile, free-draining soil, producing a crop of flowers which brighten the autumn borders without making any more demands on our time than any other quality herbaceous perennial. For years I grew a yellow-flowered, bone-hardy C. 'Jante Welles', one of the most delightful plants to grace the autumn. Unfortunately, I lost stock when changing gardens and have never been able to replace it. Such plants are well worth searching for. C. rubellum 'Clara Curtis' is one of a number of good border varieties which are still available.

The Korean hybrids will survive with no more protection than a cold frame in winter. They are produced by crossing C. coreanum with a pink-flowered Pompon variety, and are delightfully compact perennials of 18 to 24 inches (46 to 61 cm), producing a profusion of flower sprays into late autumn. I grew the Otley Koreans for years, treating them like any other hardy perennial, lifting and dividing the roots as necessary, and found them excellent. The modern Koreans are less robustly hardy and need lifting indoors for the winter. Classification of the florists' varieties of chrysanthemum is usually under six, possibly now

Good border varieties
Above left:
Chrysanthemum
'Pennine Signal'
Centre:
Chrysanthemum rubellum
'Clara Curtis'
Above right:
Chrysanthemum
'Buttercup'

Right:
Chrysanthemum 'Otley Beauty'
(Korean hybrid)

Top left (Incurved):
Chrysanthemum 'Peter Doig'
Top centre (Reflexed):
Chrysanthemum 'Joyce Stevenson'
Top right (Single-flowered):
Chrysanthemum 'Pennine Serene'
Left (Intermediate):
Chrysanthemum 'Bill Wade'

Below (Pompon):
Chrysanthemum 'Rosebud'
Below right (Double-flowered):
Chrysanthemum 'Amber Margaret'

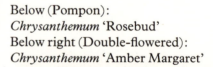

seven headings, although for show purposes these primary groups are divided into sections and sub-sections *ad infinitum*.

The seven main groups are as follows:
1 *Incurved* – where the florets curve inwards to make a perfect globe;
2 *Reflexed* – where the outer florets particularly curve upwards, partially or completely;
3 *Intermediate* – where the florets incurve loosely or irregularly;
4 *Anemone-flowered* – single but with a raised central cushion;
5 *Pompon* – small-flowered as the name implies, developed from the Chusan chrysanthemum.
6 *Singles* – varieties with no more than five rows of ray florets around a daisy centre;
7 *Miscellaneous* – this group contains a very mixed bag.

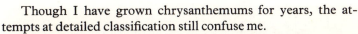

Though I have grown chrysanthemums for years, the attempts at detailed classification still confuse me.

All types of chrysanthemum are best propagated by means of cuttings. The time varies according to type. Roots are lifted from selected varieties once the flowers have faded, then stored in a frost-free place. These are started into growth, usually by spraying them overhead with water as cuttings are required. The young shoots which make the best cuttings are short-jointed, 2 to 3 inches (5 to 8 cm) long. Those which come from below the soil are to be preferred to shoots which grow out of the old stem. They can be rooted in a sandy compost over bottom heat in seven to ten days, and potted off into John Innes or peat-based compost for growing on. After suitable acclimatisation, the plants are moved outdoors in late May for the summer.

If left to grow unhindered a chrysanthemum plant will continue until an embryo bud appears at the stem tip; this is called a 'natural break bud'. It usually shrivels, and side shoots develop from leaf axils down the stem to produce a number of flower buds.

By stopping the young plants when they are 6 inches (15 cm) high, and not allowing them to grow up to the natural break bud stage, the side shoots develop from the axils much earlier. By restricting the number of side shoots and thinning the flower buds down to one per stem, the resulting blooms are much larger and of better form than if all buds were permitted to open. With some varieties, better-quality flowers are produced by stopping not only the main stem, but also the side shoots (first crown) allowing a second lot of shoots to break; this is called 'second crown flowering'. The time it takes for a plant to produce buds after the first stop is about eight weeks: if the stop is made in May, flowers will bloom in late July or August. The second stop provides a further seven- or eight-week delay; the plants so treated will flower in a heated greenhouse in November to December.

One important point to note is that the flower buds which form at the various stages (that is, natural breaks, first or second crown), develop into very different flowers depending on the number of ray florets produced. Usually when buying new plants from a nurseryman a list of instructions is supplied for each variety – whether to flower on natural break, first or second crown. This is not something it is nice to know, but MUST be known if top-quality blooms are the aim.

Development of the chrysanthemum flower bud is also influenced by day length. Only when subject to a certain number of hours of darkness do the buds develop – the chrysanthemum is what is termed a 'short-day plant', flowering in autumn. It can be persuaded to flower in spring or summer by keeping it under black polythene covers for a set number of hours. Cuttings treated with a chemical which restricts the distance between leaf joints in order to keep the plants dwarf, and then subjected to the dark treatment make excellent pot plants for home decoration – just another facet of the commercial exploitation of a very popular flower.

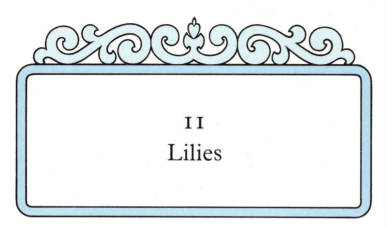

I I
Lilies

The origins of so many garden plants are rooted in the mists of ancient civilisations. When and for what reason they were first cultivated is largely a matter of conjecture.

In the first century A.D., Pliny the Elder wrote in his *Natural History* that next to the rose there is no fairer flower or one of greater estimation than the lily. Pliny was, in fact, writing of a flower whose beauty had been appreciated for 2,500 years before he was born. Down through man's history the lily story can be traced. A fragment from a Cretan vase carries a lily flower motif. Assyrian architecture appreciates and records their beauty in stone. Greek and Roman writers extol the white flowers as an emblem of purity. *Lilium candidum*, the Madonna lily was, to early medieval writers and theologians, the celestial flower-emblem of St John the Baptist.

Lily bulbs made into a bread have been eaten by those suffering from dropsy, and the flowers infused in oil were applied to tumours. The petals when steeped in brandy were reputed to have powerful healing properties, and infusions of bulbs or petals were also prescribed in the treatment of coughs and asthma. Important though all these qualities must have been when medicine relied greatly on faith and little on science, it is as a garden flower that the lily has held a secure place over many centuries.

Precisely how many species of *Lilium* there are in cultivation is difficult to discover. A loose estimate of those native to temperate regions in the Northern Hemisphere would be between eighty and a hundred. Lilies are amongst the most beautiful of bulbous plants, though, as would be expected in so large a family with a wide diversity of habitats, not all of them are easily grown under garden conditions.

Most of the species grow in climates where the seasons are well defined – cold winters, a steady progression through spring to a dry summer with very hot sunshine. The bulbs are safe in winter under a covering of snow, then, during summer's drought, they are insulated by a mulch of rotting plant debris, their roots in many cases fed by moisture which percolates through the soil from melting snow. Indeed, when comparing the climate in this country with that enjoyed by lilies in their

Lilium candidum, the Madonna lily, in northern Greece

native habitat, it is surprising that so many of them survive and flourish.

In my experience, shelter is absolutely essential; lilies, more than most plants, detest being teased about by the wind or desiccated by draughts. A free-draining, lime-free soil which never dries out even in the hottest summer provides exactly the right root conditions. This is a situation I struggled to achieve on a heavy clay soil without success. Eventually, by raising the general level some 12 inches (30 cm) above that of the surrounding soil I provided conditions in which I grew over forty species and varieties very well. Given good drainage, most soils which are lime-free when prepared with generous dressings of humus in the form of rotted manure, peat, leaf mould, shredded bark or similar rottable material will grow lilies of quality. The ideal would be if the site sloped gently south west. A deep bed

Asiatic and oriental hybrid lilies in a summer garden in Oregon

Right: *Lilium bulbiferum croceum*

of humus topped up with 12 inches (30 cm) of sandy loam would grow any but the greenhouse lilies.

In areas where the soil is alkaline, the choice should be restricted to those species which are tolerant of lime and, indeed, there are a good number of these including such established favourites as *L. candidum*, *L. regale*, *L. martagon*, and *L. monadelphum*. *L. candidum*, the Madonna lily, is one of the oldest in cultivation, being featured on vases dating from the Minoan period. Where the Madonna lily originally came from is not certain, but it seems to be so well established in the Balkan Peninsula that this could be the natural home of this lovely lily. Hundreds of years before the birth of Christ it was being cultivated as a medicinal plant. No doubt, traders distributed bulbs throughout the Mediterranean region and, wherever it found conditions congenial, colonies grew. Thus it is now found as a garden escape in several regions of the Mediterranean. The conquering armies of Rome carried the bulbs to the furthest outposts of a vast empire once policed by the legions – possibly even to Great Britain where the Venerable Bede in his writings used it as a symbol of the Resurrection.

The monks of the Middle Ages cultivated *L. candidum* in their physic gardens alongside other medicinal plants. It is one of the hardiest, most easily cultivated of lilies, given conditions to suit it, though it is one of the species which defies exact definitions of cultivation. All that the optimistic gardener can do is plant the bulbs in late August into a lime soil – not too deeply, no more than 2 inches (5 cm) of loose soil above them. Within a few weeks basal leaves grow from scales in the centre of the bulb and, once established, it should be left undisturbed. Low-growing shrubs can be planted to supply root shade while still permitting the flowers to reach up to the sunlight. Only certain forms of the Madonna lily have ever seeded in my garden, and then only sparsely, in spite of my hand-pollination when the flowers appeared in early summer.

Lilium bulbiferum croceum, the orange lily, is a native of Savoy, Corsica, and Lombardy, and is a robust, easily grown bulb. The only difference that I can discover between this variety and *L. bulbiferum* is that of colour. The former has orange-petalled flowers, while those of *L. bulbiferum* have a distinct yellow overtone to the orange. Both will thrive in any ordinary garden soil, whether acid or alkaline, providing that the drainage is good. For centuries the orange lily has enjoyed the sort of popularity that only a tolerant, easily grown plant achieves. When left alone, it will in time form strong, well-flowered colonies. Both *L. bulbiferum croceum* and *L. bulbiferum*, unlike *L. candidum* which roots from the base of the bulb only, produce roots on the stem. This dual system of rooting is why so much importance is attached to making certain all lily bulbs are planted at the proper depth. The species that root from the base of the bulb only should be shallowly planted. Those that root from the base and from that part of the stem immediately above the bulbs need to be planted deeper – 5 inches (12.5 cm) or more instead of the 2 inches (5 cm) of a basal rooting type.

Above: *Lilium columbianum* in Oregon
Below: *Lilium* 'Shuksan' at the Savill gardens

Above: *Lilium pardalinum*
Below: *Lilium martagon*

Above: *Lilium albanicum*
Below: *Lilium pyrenaicum*

For *L. bulbiferum croceum* and *L. bulbiferum* a depth of 5 inches (12 cm) would be sufficient.

The various species of lilies I have seen growing in the wild, include *L. pardalinum* and *L. columbianum*. I found *L. pardalinum* growing on a sunbaked hillside in California. Its versatility is demonstrated by the fact that I also saw the same species growing in the giant redwood forests in the northern part of this state. *L. pardalinum* is a part-parent of the Bellingham hybrids, which do so well at the Savill gardens. *L. columbianum* also has its home in N. America, and I found this high up on a hillside in Oregon. All species seem to enjoy close association with other plants, be they trees or shrubs. These give protection, particularly to the young flowering stems early in the growing season. Then, in due course, the debris of falling leaves forms a protective mulch which rots to enrich the soil.

There is a probability that the Turk's-cap, *L. martagon* is a native of this country. A colony which I saw in Devon some years ago, growing wild in rough grass alongside a copse, looked very much at home. The evidence is by no means conclusive – early writers on the subject describe it as a native of mainland Europe. *L. martagon* is the most widely distributed of all the species, its range extends from Portugal through Europe to Siberia, Turkestan, and Mongolia. As would be expected, the variations in soils over such a wide area must be enormous, and this is reflected in the way *L. martagon* has adapted to garden conditions. They are remarkable in the arrangement of the numerous dark green leaves, usually in the form of whorls round the stem. The flower stem can be anything up to 6 feet (1.8 m) in height. The pendulous flowers with turned-back petals and conspicuously protruding stamens are usually purple, but varieties are available with white, pink, red-purple, and almost black flowers – from three to as many as forty to a stem. Of all the *L. martagon* varieties, those with pure white flowers and dark green foliage are the most pleasing. The roots form at the base of the bulb, so they should be planted no more than 3 to 4 inches (7.5 to 10 cm) deep.

Another species which I find most attractive is *L. albanicum*. As its name suggests, it is to be found in southern Europe. Last year I found it growing on the edge of a pine forest in northern Greece quite near the border with Albania. Standing anything between 2 and 4 feet (0.6 to 1.2 m) high, it carried the most delicate yellow flowers.

Scent, like beauty, is in the nose or eyes of the recipient, for *L. pyrenaicum* and, indeed, *L. martagon* are described as having a foul odour. Possibly because my memories of both these easily cultivated lilies are of seeing them in the most pleasant of circumstances I may be biassed, for the scent to me is pleasant enough. Of the early writers, John Parkinson is the first to depict what he describes as the yellow Turk's-cap, so *L. pyrenaicum* is a late sixteenth- or early seventeenth-century introduction. This is surprising, for an easy-going species, native to the Pyrénées, is almost local when compared to the Madonna lily. Very easy to grow, the base-rooting bulbs planted 4 inches (10 cm) deep soon establish to push up greenish-yellow flowers with brown spots and brilliant orange anthers on stems 3 feet (90 cm) high in June.

The bright orange flowers of the tiger lily, flaunting themselves against the shiny waxen leaves of a laurel hedge in August, were such an accepted part of life's pattern that they conditioned me into thinking of *L. tigrinum* as one of the older species in cultivation. In fact, bulbs were sent to Kew from China in 1804. The Chinese grew them as a farm crop for the sake of the bulbs, which are edible. It is a stem-rooting lily which needs planting 6 inches (15 cm) deep. The orange-red petals curl back to show a purple spotted interior. A form, introduced by Robert Fortune from Korea in 1850, grows taller, with stems covered in a cottony pubescence and bearing from twenty to thirty large flowers.

Another species from the Far East which has won favour with indoor gardeners is the Easter lily, *L. longiflorum*. This has its origins in Japan. Its long, white, trumpet-shaped flowers and its ability to be forced easily make it a very popular house plant.

Lilium longiflorum

In his book *The Lilies of Eastern Asia*, E. H. Wilson, the plant hunter who introduced *L. regale*, writes: 'This lily has a surprisingly limited distribution, being confined to about fifty miles of the narrow semi-arid valley of the Min River in extreme Western Szechuan, between 2500 and 6000 ft [750 and 1800m] altitude – a region where the summers are hot and the winters are cold. From the last week in April to the first week in July, according to altitude the blossoms of this lily transform a desolate, lonely region into a veritable garden of beauty, and its fragrance fills the air.'

Along the valley, according to Wilson's report, the lily is plentiful, growing among grasses and low shrubs. So far as is known at the present time, this wild, lonely valley of the Min river is the only place where *L. regale* grows wild. Mr E. H. Wilson sent home bulbs to the nursery firm of Messrs Vietch in 1904. It was one of the most important plant introductions of his career, for this, one of the loveliest of lilies, has been a major influence in the breeding of new varieties. The slender, flexible, yet strong flower stems grow 3 to 4 feet (0.9 to 1.2 m) tall and are crowned by a number of funnel-shaped blooms. These are shaded brown, fading to pink on the outside, while the inside is yellow in the centre graduating to pure white at the rim. It is a superb lily for the garden – the bulbs can be planted in the autumn or spring, 6 inches (15 cm) deep, as they are stem-rooting. New stock can be grown from seed for flowering in two years, thus amassing large quantities of bulbs for growing in pots, or for general planting.

Though *L. auratum*, the golden-rayed lily of Japan, was brought to this country by Mr J. G. Vietch some forty years before *L. regale* and caused something of a sensation when exhibited, it has not the same sound constitution and perennial qualities. Maybe the plant's immediate popularity led to over-production, for it quickly becomes infected with a weakening

Top right: *Lilium regale*
Below right: *Lilium auratum*

virus disease. In Japan it grows wild in areas ranging from Honshu to the north, and down into Hokkondo in the south west. One form grows in volcanic detritus on the slopes of Mount Fuji Yama – a condition it would be hard to reproduce in a garden. Though *L. auratum* is virus-prone, it has made a most important contribution as a parent of numerous hybrids. Once again, it is Mr E. F. Wilson who, after seeing them growing in the wild, gives the soundest advice on their cultivation. Healthy bulbs planted from 8 to 12 inches (20 to 30 cm) deep in not-too-fertile, lime-free soil where the drainage is perfect and amongst shrubs which protect the young growth from sunlight, will thrive as they do on their native heath. I grew several varieties of *L. auratum* in open woodland amongst azaleas whose roots ensured that no surplus moisture lingered overlong, and they flowered well for eight years. Deep planting is important, as this is a stem-rooting species, and an annual top dressing of leaf-mould will be beneficial. The flowers are large, often 12 inches (30 cm) across, and carried in profusion on tall stems. Ivory white in colour, they are spotted maroon to red and with a distinct gold bar down each petal. Add to the superb flower a fragrance which rejoices the garden from July to October if several varieties are planted, and this lily becomes a paragon of garden plants.

Ranking with the golden-rayed lily in popularity and importance to the plant hybridist, *L. speciosum* is a species of singular charm. Whereas *L. auratum*, in my experience, produces few if any secondary bulbs, *L. speciosum* will establish thriving colonies given the right soil conditions. The native home of *L. speciosum* is given by some authorities as south Japan and, indeed, it is grown extensively in Japanese nurseries, whereas others give the hills of central China as the point of origin. The name *speciosum*, meaning showy or splendid, aptly describes the flamboyant, brilliance of the flowers. One of the latest to come into bloom in northern gardens – September to October – it makes a splendid complement to the autumn colour of maples and Sargent's cherry. Bulbs can be planted in the autumn, or potted up and then moved out in spring. As stem rooters, they need to go down deep, even 8 inches (20 cm) is not too much in well-prepared soil. Widely reflexing flowers which measure 6 inches (15 cm) or more across are carried on 3- to 5-foot (0.9- to 1.5-m) stems. These are a carmine red on an ivory-white background, and they are delightfully but not overpoweringly fragrant. Many varieties exist of this quite variable lily, plus an ever-increasing selection of hybrids. Another attractive and relatively recent addition is *L. mackliniae* from Manipur. This species is easily raised from seed.

One of the best known North American species, *L. canadense* grows in meadows and marshy places – the sort of conditions most gardeners would be reluctant to provide. Bulbs of this most attractive lily, which I planted in moist soil amongst azaleas, increased steadily into a thriving, well-flowered colony. Regular mulching with leaf-mould supplied a sufficiently cool, moist root run. The bulbs are rhizomatous (the new bulb grows on the end of a scaly underground stem) and should be planted 8 inches (20 cm) deep. Bell-shaped flowers which appear on 4- to 5-foot (1.2- to 1.5-m) high stems in June vary in colour from yellow, through orange to red.

There is so much variation in both flower form and colour amongst the species, that exploring all the attributes lends extra interest to the growing of these plants.

Far left: *Lilium mackliniae*
Left: *Lilium monadelphum szovitsianum*

The author in an Oregon bulb field with *Lilium* 'Gold Medal'

From the Caucasus, the amiable *L. monadelphum szovitsianum* is one I have grown for many years, for it is a beautiful form. Stems 5 to 6 feet (1.5 to 1.8 m) high carry from ten to twenty deep yellow, waxy, fragrant flowers which open in June. The bulbs should be planted 5 inches (12.5 cm) deep amongst deciduous shrubs in a west facing border.

Central China has provided so many exceptional species that I am always persuaded to try and accommodate any which come my way. *L. henryi*, sometimes called the orange speciosum, will grow in most soils including those containing lime. Listed as growing only 5 feet (1.5 m) high in the wild, in cultivation it sometimes tops 8 feet (2.4 m) with up to twenty orange-coloured flowers per stem in July and August. It is a stem-rooting species, so the bulbs are planted 6 to 8 inches (15 to 20 cm deep.

Hybridising between the species has resulted in variations which are bewildering in their complexity, and in some cases

aggressively violent in flower colour. The first hybrid was the result of a natural cross-pollination between *L. candidum* and the bright orange-scarlet *L. chalcedonicum* which, surprisingly turned up in a package of *L. martagon* bulbs. The hybrid bloomed in 1838, the dark apricot petals reflexing to show contrasting orange anthers. Called *L. × testaceum*, this is a lovely lily which will tolerate a lime soil. As with *L. candidum*, it is base-rooting, so it should be covered with no more than 2 inches (5 cm) of soil.

The first hybrid was followed by imports from Japan of a race of garden lilies now grouped under *L. × maculatum*, and these are, in my experience, the most tolerant and easily cultivated of all lilies. They are the earliest to flower – in June most years – displaying ample heads of upward facing flowers. The bulbs are large and should be planted 6 to 8 inches (15 to 20 cm) deep where the flower stems can be seen against a dark foliaged shrub. All are compact in height growing up to 3 feet (90 cm) or possibly an inch or two more in good soil. The flowers can be in shades of yellow, orange, or crimson. Most of those I grow are orange-crimson and flower very freely. *L. × hollandicum* includes *L. maculatum* in its parentage, with the same colour range, but with me the flowers open a little later in July.

In recent years, skilful, world-wide cross-pollination has resulted in the introduction of an ever-increasing range of hybrids. The bulb fields of Oregon have yielded robust, floriferous perennials which even the complete gardening novice should find pleasantly easy to grow.

Above:
Lilium 'Impact' (Asiatic)
Top right:
Lilium 'Black Dragon' (Trumpet)
Centre right:
Lilium 'Edith' (Asiatic) at an Oregon bulb farm
Below right:
An unnamed hybrid of Dr Chris North

Below: *Lilium chalcedonicum*

'Enchantment' is excellent both in the garden and as a pot plant. A single bulb can produce 30- to 36-inch (75- to 90-cm) high stems with a dozen or more large, bright orange, outward facing flowers – usually in July. 'Edith' is of similar character though with flowers of pale primrose yellow. 'Impact', with flowers of even brighter orange than 'Enchantment', has purple stripes at the base of each petal as if some one had carefully drawn a paint brush across each bloom.

Those with a preference for the spectacularly lovely flared trumpet lilies will possibly find themselves spoiled for choice. 'Golden Splendour' has 6-inch (15-cm) wide blooms, the deep gold petals embellished with a maroon stripe on the outer side. A stem 5 feet (1.5m) high carrying six or more fully open flowers makes a lovely picture in August sunshine. 'Black Dragon' is equally imposing. The flowers 8 inches (20 cm) across are like flared trumpets, white on the inside, maroon on the reverse, with a fragrance that is discernible from a considerable distance. Sturdy stems 6 feet (1.8 m) high may support up to twenty flowers on a well grown plant.

In this country, Dr Chris North from the Invergowie Plant Breeding Research Station in Scotland has made a significant contribution to new, disease-tolerant lilies. Using *L. lankongense* as a parent with embryo culture techniques, he has brought a new dimension to the lily as a garden flower with his attractive hybrids.

Though no longer a member of the lily genus, *Cardiocrinum giganteum* was for so long the largest and tallest of the clan until botanists ordered its expulsion, that it is only proper to offer it at least a mention. The only difference between this and a true lily is in the broad, heart-shaped leaves which form in whorls near the bottom of the stem. They grow up to 8 feet (2.4 m) high, even 10 feet (3 m) in rich soil, and bear numerous creamy white, fragrant, tubular-shaped flowers. Each individual bloom is at least 6 inches (15 cm) long and is streaked with purple. The flowering season is July and August. The bulbs, which die after flowering, should be planted shallowly in the richest possible soil with the tip exposed on the surface. A heavy mulch of rotted manure or leaf-mould should be spread over the bed to protect the bulbs from frost. Though the parent bulb dies after flowering, offsets form which in due course grow and produce flowers and seed in their turn. To give an indication as to how rich the soil needs to be, one of the tasks I helped with as a gardening apprentice was the preparation of a bed prior to planting *Cardiocrinum giganteum*. The ingredients used included slaughter-house offal, beech leaf-mould, and chopped loam. When the bulbs flowered, each 10-feet (3-m) high stem carried at least twenty blooms.

Cardiocrinum giganteum

Lilium 'Midnight' (Aurelian)

Lilium 'Cover Girl' (Oriental)

Lilium × *hollandicum*

The propagation of lilies to increase stock is not difficult. Seed can be sown immediately it is ripe into a frame or into boxes which need to be at least 8 inches (20 cm) deep and filled with loam-based compost. Once germinated, the seed can be left to grow for two years before the small bulbs are transferred to a nursery border.

Lily bulbs are made up of a series of fleshy overlapping 'scales'. If these are detached carefully and inserted into John Innes or peat-based compost, they will grow a new bulb at the base. The process can be shortened if the scales are mixed with peat, then placed in a polythene bag, and hung in a warm, dark place – the airing cupboard is ideal. In six weeks each scale will have grown roots and can then be potted off.

Some of the lilies very obligingly grow small bulbs in leaf axils and amongst the flower heads, *L. tigrinum*, *L.* × *maculatum*, and *L. bulbiferum* are three which do this. These can be removed in early autumn and potted up in loam or a peat-based compost for growing on. Ariel bulbs are known as bulbils, and are not to be confused with bulblets which form at or below soil level. Bulblets appear in many varieties on the underground section of the stem, just above the bulb, and these can also be removed without disturbing the bulb, and potted up.

There are lilies – *L.* × *maculatum*, *L. bulbiferum croceum*, and *L. candidum* which, having had the flower stem pulled from the old bulb as the flowers fade, and being laid in a compost of equal parts loam, peat and sand, will form small bulblets on the stem, usually near where the stem was pulled from the old bulb.

Division is an obvious method of increasing stock, though this is only possible where the lilies are really thriving. Even then I would hesitate to lift established bulbs or disturb them any more than necessary. A few scales can be taken from each bulb without them being lifted, so this is the system I adopt.

Lilies bring a regal quality to the garden which no other flower, not even the rose can equal. Among things lovely and of good report the lily claims a place.

The Lily Group of the Royal Horticultural Society and the North American Lily Society have classified the various hybrid lilies produced from inter-specific hybridisation into eight groups:

1 Asiatics – derived from such species as *L. tigrinum* and *L. davidii* and hybrid groups such as *L.* × *hollandicum* and *L.* × *maculatum*.
2 Martagons – hybrids of *L. martagon* or *L. hansonii* with Turk's-cap flowers.
3 Hybrids derived from *L. candidum*, *L. chalcedonicum* and other related European species, but excluding *L. martagon*.
4 Hybrids of American species.
5 Hybrids derived from *L. longiflorum* and *L. formosanum*.
6 Trumpet-flowered Aurelian hybrids.
7 Orientals – derived from species such as *L. auratum*, *L. speciosum*, *L. japonicum* etc.
8 Hybrids not classified elsewhere.

12
Violas

Most of the world's plants have no common names, they are known only by a botanical or Latin designation. Quite naturally, before a system of botanical nomenclature was devised, country folk contrived names to identify any plant which was of interest, either in economic, medicinal, religious, or aesthetic terms. Sometimes the original, popular name for a plant is incorporated into the botanical title. Occasionally a popular name is adopted from another language. The pansy, known for constancy and remembrance in British folk lore derives from a French word *pensée*, meaning *thought*. Few of our native flowers enjoy the affectionate esteem bestowed on the wild pansy, *Viola tricolor*, and this is reflected in the multiplicity of common names – at the time of writing I have discovered sixteen. My favourites are heart's-ease, kiss-me-at-the-garden-gate, and tittle-my-fancy.

The family is a large one, for over five hundred species are contained within the genus *Viola*. Some are annuals, while

Modern hybrid pansies and
a wild violet

Far left: *Viola tricolor*
Left: *Viola odorata* (white form)

others, including the species cultivated as garden plants, are short-lived perennials for the most part. The best known are *V. odorata*, sweet violet, and *V. tricolor* – ancestor of the pansy. The race of hybrids bred from *V. tricolor*, assisted by crosses from other species are grouped for convenience under *Viola × wittrockiana*.

Oldest in cultivation is sweet violet which has flowers in shades of purple and white. This was grown for sale as a cut flower in Greek markets four hundred years before the birth of Christ. Ion, the Greek name for the violet, is reputed to have been bestowed on the flower by Jupiter when he changed Io, daughter of the King of Argos with whom he fell in love, into a white heifer, so as to conceal her from the jealousy of his wife Hera. Jupiter then caused sweet violets to spring from the earth, thus providing herbage worthy of her beauty.

In eastern countries the violet, possibly *V. alba* not our native *V. odorata*, enjoys enormous prestige. Sherbet flavoured with the blossom was a popular drink at Arabian banquets. The Persian adage 'The excellence of the violet is as the excellence of El Islam above all other religions', indicates the regard, almost reverence, in which the flower was held. Romans also held violets in high esteem, cultivating them in gardens, and using the flowers to fashion garlands for a favourite poet or bard. The blooms were also used for making wine, a curious competitor, indeed, for the beverage fermented from the grape. In Britain the violet was an emblem of constancy. To quote from an old sonnet 'Violets is for faithfulness, which in me shall abide'.

Violet flowers were much used as a flavouring in confectionery and are still sold coated with sugar and gum arabic as cake decorations. I find it puzzling that the violet was not used in the perfume trade until the very late eighteenth century. Possibly the essence proved difficult to extract and fix, or substances such as orris, made from the rhizome of an iris, offered a cheaper alternative. The violet, along with the rose, was a favourite flower of the Empress Josephine, wife of Napoleon, who cultivated the plants in her famous garden at Malmaison. Roses are still grown in the garden there, though search as I might only one small clump of violets revealed itself growing wild in the shade of trees beside the lake. Violets, their popularity stimulated by royal patronage, were cultivated intensively in gardens near Paris for sale in the city. In southern France violets were grown on a field scale for the perfume which could be extracted from the flowers, and for export to the London market.

In England the growing of violets on a commercial scale was mostly confined to the Avon valley where the flowers were used in the manufacture of a chemical called Syrup of Violets. As their attractiveness as a cut flower grew, nurseries specialising in violet culture began to appear near several major cities, particularly London but also Bath and Bristol.

Though our native sweet violet has been cultivated in gardens for centuries and has given rise to a quantity of natural mutations or 'sports', the modern varieties are the result of crosses between several species. *V. cyanea* from Russia with fragrant blue or violet flowers is one of the 'stud' species.

Below left: *Viola* 'Perle Rose'
Below: *Viola* 'St Helena'

Viola 'Duchesse de Parme'

Another is *V. suavis* which in the wild ranges from Russia through Turkey to Kashmir. I grow this species, or one closely akin to it, as *V. pontica*; it carries large pale blue flowers with a white eye and distills a pleasing fragrance. Last though certainly not least in importance, and again much like sweet violet in appearance, is *V. alba*, with white, violet, and all shades between, including rose and reddish-purple, sweetly-scented flowers. The 'Czar' which has the distinction of being the first violet to gain an award from the Royal Horticultural Society, raised in 1863 at Cranford in Middlesex, was a Russian seedling. Growers from then on introduced a whole range of new hybrids with the 'Czar' as one parent. 'Princess of Wales' with rich violet flowers on long stems, 'St Helena' in pale lavender-blue, 'Perle Rose' and 'Duchesse de Parme' are four notable names from a very long list.

The Parma violets, though they have been grown in this country for over a century are a beautiful, difficult to cultivate

Viola lutea

mystery, whose origins are uncertain. They did, however, achieve an immense popularity with a perfume which once enjoyed is never forgotten, and is, I think, different in the musk rose overtone to that of the sweet violet. I have only been able to grow these under northern conditions in a cold frame; possibly elsewhere they will survive outdoors.

A deep, fertile, well-drained, slightly alkaline soil will usually grow violets well. Before planting it is advisable to dig in a liberal dressing of well-rotted farm manure, compost, or leaf-mould so that the soil is moisture-retentive yet porous enough for the roots to penetrate easily.

Runners or roots may be planted in spring with the crown of the plant just resting fractionally above soil level. Once the roots are established, remove any runners which grow from the centre to concentrate all the plant's energy into flower production.

The popular pansy is, compared to the violet, a native with a well-recorded history. Fortunately, the man who began by hybridisation and selection to improve the flower quality of the garden pansy, *V.* × *wittrockiana*, was that uncommon combination of gardener, plant breeder, and author – a man called Thompson, gardener to Lord Gambier. Starting with the yellow and white heart's-ease about 1814, Mr Thompson began to select those of his raised seedlings which showed improved flower size and colour variation. Encouraged by the results, he gathered together all the varieties in commerce. The annual *V. tricolor*, perennial *V. lutea*, and possibly the Russian species were all entered into the breeding line. As so frequently happens, the first blotched or 'puss-faced' variety appeared as

Right: a modern hybrid pansy

a self-sown seedling growing amongst heathers. This foundling was restored to its rightful place in the pansy yard, and within another fifteen years the new strain had become 'show' flowers. Even the classification was exact, as it must still be today, for exhibition purposes – 'self-coloured' with petals all one shade, though a contrasting eye was acceptable. Other classes included a single ground colour, white or yellow for the lower petals, with the two upper petals of a differing hue. Interest in the pansy quickened with importation from French and Dutch nurseries of a new strain of pansies which were called 'Fancy' to differentiate them from the already admired Show Pansies. In more recent times, selection has given us 'Dream French Giants', which have no face and come in a wide range of colours.

Gardeners are slow to accept change, and almost a decade passed before the new strain achieved acknowledgment. Now, of course, it is the Show Pansy which is the laggard in popularity. Crosses between *V. lutea*, *V. tricolor*, *V. amoena*, and in the last quarter of the nineteenth century *V. cornuta*, combined to give both garden and bedding pansies a quality which would have delighted Mr Thompson, the man they called 'Father of the heart's-ease'. The description applied to pansies then is still true today. They are inexpensive, easily managed, and beautiful. Botanists group viola, tufted pansy, and violettas (derived from crossing garden pansies with *V. cornuta*) under the title *V. × williamsi* – *V. × wittrockiana* covers the garden pansy.

The cultivation of the summer flowering varieties, 'Clear Crystal', 'Prince Henry', 'Giant', and 'Roggli' strains, plus the named varieties of tufted pansy, old favourites like 'Maggie Mott' and 'Irish Molly', is similar. A good, fertile, well-drained soil which will not become excessively dry in summer or wet in

Top and above:
'Dream French Giant' pansies

Opposite
Top: *Viola* 'Prince Henry'
Centre: *Viola cornuta*
Below: *Viola biflora*

winter, and sunny or partially shaded borders will suit all varieties. Seed sown in July will produce plants large enough to go outside in their flowering positions by September. Alternatively, seed may be sown under glass in March for planting outdoors in May. All the species and varieties can be propagated by cuttings made from non-flowering basal shoots during the summer months.

Though the species do not enjoy the universal acclaim of the larger-flowered, brighter-coloured hybrids, several are very worthy of garden cultivation. *V. cornuta*, mentioned previously as playing an important part as progenitor of the pansy cum viola, was introduced from the Pyrenees late in the eighteenth century. Conditions in some areas have proved so congenial that it has escaped to become naturalised. The large pale violet flowers open on 10-inch (25-cm) high stems, but there is a white form which occurs naturally when fresh stock is raised from seed. It is an excellent ground cover plant flowering in early summer, then again in early July if the clusters are trimmed with shears. A variety of *V. cornuta* which I grow, called 'Campanula Blue', has lavender-coloured flowers and is a prime perennial.

Another alpine favourite is *V. biflora* with clear, yellow flowers and kidney-shaped leaves. It peeps brightly from beneath and between rocks where it finds sufficient shelter. Much more of a challenge to the gardener's skill is *V. jaubertiana*, which I find does best in an alpine trough.

Some of the species are very tiny, but their elfin charm hides a cast-iron durability. *V. saxatilis aetolica*, or as some catalogues list it – just plain *V. aetolica*, only grows to 2 or 3 inches (5 to 8 cm) high. The pansy-like yellow flowers measure an inch (2.5 cm) across in the best forms. I have grown it amongst dwarf, blue-blossomed rhododendrons which flowered with the viola in April and May. Of the viola species I have grown, *V. cucullata* from North America is one of the most excellent perennials. Heart-shaped, pale green leaves provide the back-cloth to inch-wide flowers, varying in shade from white through violet to lavender. *V. beckwithii*, a North American species from Oregon, has two violet upper petals and three lilac lower petals – an ideal natural complement.

There is a tendency for some of the species to be so over-shadowed by their more aggressively coloured offspring that they are lost to cultivation, and *V. gracilis* is such a one. I grew my plants from seed, and used them as ground cover over bulbs and hardy cyclamen in a frame. The purple flowers opened in March through to June in a pleasant association with those of bulbs. The species *V. glabella* that I found growing in woodland at the Chelsea Physic Garden in London came originally from the west of North America. In dappled sunlight it seemed to reflect all the delicate charm of the family.

Some species are capable of growing in shady places under trees or on the north side of buildings, and *V. labradorica* is use-ful in this respect. I grow the form with purple foliage as ground cover in a shade border in company with ferns, dog's-tooth violet and similar plants. There, this viola from North America and Greenland makes a carpet of foliage, starred in spring with mauve flowers borne on 4-inch (10-cm) high stems. When well suited it can be invasive, demanding more than a fair share of space. As would be expected, seed forms the easiest means of raising fresh stock.

Meeting a plant on its own native heath tends to leave an indelible imprint on the memory. Seeing the common dog violet, *V. riviniana* growing in company with primroses on the steeply sloping bank of a stream on a Yorkshire fellside made a lasting impression on my mind. The carpet of violet flowers with primroses growing amongst them, and the soft greenness of spring lying overall had a wild, captivating beauty. Another lasting memory is of *V. canina* growing on a bank in the grounds of Rievaulx Abbey.

Viola jaubertiana

Below left: *Viola beckwithii*
Below: *Viola glabella*

Above: *Viola canina*
Right: *Viola* 'Huntercombe Purple'

Viola riviniana

V. zoysii is another native I took a liking to when walking in the east European Alps. It has dark foliage and clear yellow flowers.

Were it not so lovely, the bird's-foot violet, *V. pedata* would be dismissed as too difficult and temperamental. I have found it quite content when planted in very sandy soil over a bed of leaf-mould, once the slugs have been persuaded to refrain from devouring it. There, the light blue violet flowers opened in succession during late April and May on 4-inch (10-cm) stems.

Though the mountain pansy, *V. lutea*, is ancestor to many garden hybrids, it is also one of the prettiest of our native flowers and as such warrants more than just a passing mention. I have seen hillsides where the grass was bejewelled with mountain pansy flowers, mostly yellow, but with a proportion of blue forms, and others a mixture of the two colours. For garden purposes, of course, the hybrids are better value, though I cherish a small colony for the memories the flowers conjure up.

V. tricolor, the little yellow and dark blue flowered annual, known as heart's-ease, seeds itself cheerfully around the garden into any cranny which offers root hold. In poor soils it is neat and compact at only 2 inches (5 cm) high, but given more fertile root run it spreads luxuriantly into a mat 15 inches (38 cm) across and up to 8 inches (20 cm) high.

Hybrids of the pansy derived from *V. tricolor* show their origins if allowed to seed about the garden. Each succeeding generation reverts more nearly to the parent characteristics. There is a subspecies of *V. tricolor*, called *macedonica*, which will grace any garden. Like the species, it flowers all summer through, but its petals are a cheerful dark red. Though only a short-lived annual, self-sown seedlings spring up to fill the space left vacant.

The generous family of violets offers so much choice to the gardener that it is churlish not to provide them bed and board in return for the pleasure they give.

13
Fuchsias

Of the hundred or so species of fuchsia identified at the present time ninety-four are natives of Central and South America, four grow naturally in New Zealand, and one grows wild in Tahiti. The genus is named after Leonhard Fuchs, a German professor, physician, and herbalist, whose great work was a book on medicinal plants illustrated with beautiful woodcuts.

Although to the layman's eye there is no similarity between the plants, in their botanical classification fuchsias are grouped in the same family as the evening primrose, willow herb, and godetia. In 1693 Charles Plumier, a French missionary and botanist, discovered on San Domingo a plant he called *Fuchsia triphylla flore coccineo*. In a book he published during 1703, Plumier describes and illustrates the fuchsia he discovered ten years previously. The genus was founded and given botanical classification by Linnaeus in 1753 on the information provided by Father Plumier.

Seeds of the newly discovered fuchsia were sent to Philip Miller, curator of the Chelsea Physic Garden, from Cartagena in Colombia by Dr Houstoun, a Scottish surgeon, who collected plants in Central America and the West Indies. Dr Houstoun also made notes and drawings of the plants he found, so the event is well recorded. Precisely when the seeds were sent is not clear, but as Miller was not made curator until 1722, and Dr Houstoun died in 1733 it must have been during that period.

Fuchsia triphylla is described as a semi-shrubby plant growing from 10 to 20 inches (25 to 50 cm) high with leathery copper-bronze leaves. The flowers have a long, cinnabar-red tube fading at the base, and short petals. As would be expected, *F. triphylla* cannot survive frost or winter temperatures below 40°F. (4°C.). This probably explains why it soon disappeared from cultivation and was not mentioned or seen again, in garden terms that is, for more than a hundred years.

The next recorded species to be found, *F. coccinea*, was again discovered by a French missionary, R. Feuillée, who described it in his book on Chilean plants first published in 1714. The Royal Botanic Gardens at Kew were presented with a plant of *F. coccinea* in 1788 by Captain Firth. There is some difference of opinion amongst writers on the history of the

Fuchsia 'Gartenmeister Bonstedt'

Left: *Fuchsia coccinea*

fuchsia as to whether seed of *F. triphylla* was grown to flowering from the 1722–33 introductions. In the event that the attempt failed, then *F. coccinea* was the first species to be seen growing in this country. Described as a slender branched shrub up to 3 feet (90 cm) in height, it has solitary flowers borne in the upper leaf axils, with a red tube and sepals complemented by a violet to purple corolla. Though the true species is now rare in cultivation, it is of considerable importance having had a major influence in the breeding of new fuchsia hybrids.

Almost at the same time, possibly brought in on the same ship that delivered *F. coccinea*, came *F. magellanica*, adding the first hint of mystery and romance to the fuchsia story. The tale runs that James Lee, a nurseryman of Hammersmith, was showing a prospective customer around his stock, and the visitor, seemingly unimpressed, passed a comment that he had

Left: *Fuchsia magellanica* 'Alba'
Above: *Fuchsia magellanica* in
the west coast of Ireland

seen a better plant growing in the window of a house in Wapping. James Lee reacted to this unsolicited piece of information quite predictably by rushing off in search of this paragon of plants, and discovered it to be a fuchsia different to any he had seen. According to the lady, her sailor husband had brought it back from the West Indies. By emptying his pockets of all the cash he had on him, Lee persuaded the woman to part, somewhat reluctantly, with her plant. So, for a total of about eight guineas and a promise that she should also have two of the first cuttings propagated, the woman gave up the prize. The plant, at first wrongly identified as *F. coccinea*, was in truth *F. magellanica*. Fittingly, there is a good plant *F. magellanica* 'Alba' on display at the Chelsea Physic Garden in London.

Those less romantically inclined cast grave doubts on the story. Neither *F. coccinea* or *F. magellanica* is native to the West Indies. Did Lee receive it from one of his own collectors? Did he, as some suggest, invent the story to cover up the acquisition of cuttings from Kew Gardens to account for its being in his possession. No one can now discern truth from fiction. One thing is certain, that in 1793 Lee sold large numbers of fuchsias at considerable profit to himself – reports say the charge was one guinea per plant – a handsome sum indeed.

F. magellanica is native to Chile and Argentina, and is a tall-growing hardy shrub with graceful flowers of the elegant, classic form beloved by the specialists. The colour of bloom is described as tube red, sepals deep red, and corolla purple. In spite of all the stories surrounding its introduction, botanical sources insist there is no evidence of the species being grown in Great Britain prior to 1820. In the wild state *F. magellanica* grows in moist, sometimes marshy ground, which is confirmed by the preference shown in cultivation for areas of high rainfall. In Ireland, the Isle of Man and in Cornwall, hedges of *F.*

Right: *Fuchsia thymifolia* in Mexico

magellanica grow 8 feet (2.4 m) or more in moist, humid conditions. Being hardy, a trait passed on frequently to its offspring, *F. magellanica* is an important stud plant to the hybridist.

In 1827 *F. thymifolia* arrived from Mexico and the next fifty years saw, if not a flood of new introductions, at least what could be described as a constant trickle. *F. lycioides*, brought at the beginning of the nineteenth century from Chile, is a 9-foot (2.7-m) high shrub and fairly hardy, the flower colour – tube red, petals purple. About the same time *F. decussata*, *F. corymbiflora*, *F. apetala* and *F. serratifolia* put in an appearance. Both *F. serratifolia* and *F. corymbiflora* have been used as parents to produce new hybrids. In 1841 *F. splendens* was introduced. In all, fourteen or more species were introduced in the short span of twenty years. Another was *F. microphylla* from Brazil with short stems up to 3 feet (90 cm) high and small dark red and rose

Fuchsia splendens

flowers. Three years later the tree-like *F. arborescens* arrived, a native of Mexico and Panama. A variable plant, which grows sometimes as an epiphyte, a small shrub or, as the name suggests, a 25-foot (7.5-m) high tree, the flowers are not large, the tube is rose, and the corolla lilac. In Mexico I found only one bush, presumed to be *F. arborescens*, scrambling feebly amongst coarse vegetation. One that does grow in profusion in that country is *F. encliandra* which enjoys the conditions that a pine forest can offer.

These lesser members of the genus preceded the arrival of a truly noteworthy member of the family in the shape of *F. fulgens*. Sent from Mexico to the Horticultural Society in 1828, the long tubular flowers and beautiful foliage attracted immediate attention. To see a 4-foot (1.2-m) high specimen growing on a rock outcrop in open woodland with the vast panorama of the Mexican mountains beyond was an unforgettable experience. The leaves were broader than I have seen on any of the many *F. fulgens* which have graced my gardening life. The flowers were larger, bright red and fading to orange at the base. Individuals were scattered across the half mile of hillside which I explored, some interlaced with sub-shrubs, others growing alone in humus-rich, stony soil. There were differences in leaf size and flower colour which seemed to depend more on habitat than genetic variation. *F. fulgens* is reported in the Botanical Magazine for 1841 as being, in combination with other species, the means of producing a great number of hybrids. Curtis of Glazenwood, and Bunney of Stratford were two of the early practitioners in the field.

F. procumbens is a reputedly hardy species which has proved distinctly tender in my experience. It is a most un-fuchsia-like prostrate creeping shrub with wiry stems, furnished with heart-shaped leaves. The flowers are small without petals, and they have an orange-yellow calyx tube and purple leaf-like lobes. The fruit, which is the same size as the flowers, colours flesh pink. In its native New Zealand, *F. procumbens* grows in sandy or gravelly soil in coastal regions. A most unusual species, and worth a place in the collection, but I can find no record of New Zealand species hybridising with any others. The cross-fertilising has all been between *F. magellanica*, *F. coccinea*, *F. fulgens* and available species from America.

The earliest break in colour occurred in the mid-nineteenth century, when a seedling from *F. magellanica* flowered showing a white tube and bluish purple corolla. Introduced by a Tunbridge Wells Nursery as 'Venus Victrix', it offered the prospect of new, even more diverse colour variations.

In a very short space of time the fuchsia achieved a remarkable popularity, with breeders in both Great Britain and the continent of Europe, raising seedlings bred from crosses between the available species that were suitably compatible. The first book dealing entirely with fuchsia cultivation was printed in 1848 and lists 520 species and varieties. By the end of the century the number had risen to 1500, and plants were being sold in Covent Garden at the rate of 10,000 per day. One

Above: *Fuchsia arborescens*
Right: *Fuchsia fulgens* in Mexico

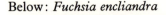

Below: *Fuchsia encliandra*

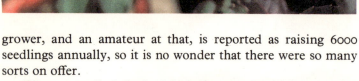

grower, and an amateur at that, is reported as raising 6000 seedlings annually, so it is no wonder that there were so many sorts on offer.

These, so-called, florists' fuchsias are too tender to survive a winter outdoors in this country, though they are used extensively for summer bedding. Instead, credit must be given to the one species, *F. magellanica* and its forms, for the race of shrubs which, even under the extremes of weather conditions inflicted on those who garden in Yorkshire Dales, have proved indestructibly hardy. From the books I have read dealing with the parentage of modern fuchsia hybrids, the two most important species are *F. fulgens* and *F. magellanica*, though other species have contributed and, no doubt, will do so increasingly in the future.

The garden fuchsias, as opposed to those which need winter protection in a greenhouse, make no great demands on the skills of those who grow them. In mild areas the hardy fuchsias make quite large, well-furnished shrubs; elsewhere top growth is frequently killed back to soil level by frost. In spring when all the dead stems are cut away, strong shoots grow from the perennial root to flower in July.

Any well drained soil will suit fuchsias. Before planting, a little rotted leaf soil, compost, or farm manure can be worked into the top twelve inches (30 cm), plus a dusting of meat and bone meal. As fuchsias root very quickly and easily from cuttings of young, non-flowering shoots taken at any time during the growing season, raising extra stock presents no problems.

Above left: *Fuchsia* 'Alice Hoffman'
Above: *Fuchsia* 'Corallina'
Below: *Fuchsia magellanica* 'Riccartonii'

Without doubt *F. magellanica* and varieties derived from it are the hardiest. In the type plant, the flowers though small are carried in such profusion that their individual size becomes unimportant. There was an enormous bush in the garden around my childhood home, and popping the tight buds to make them open became a habit in which I still absentmindedly indulge.

A pale-flowered form called *F. magellanica molinae* is the tallest I have grown, but the pale lilac petals and white tube are too insipid for my taste. There is a form of the dark red-flowered *F. magellanica gracilis* which offers a pleasant alternative to the plain-leaved sort, called 'Variegata'. The red flowers are identical with those of *F. magellanica gracilis*, but are displayed against silver foliage. Any branches which revert to plain green should be pruned away immediately they appear. Of the various forms which are not produced from crosses between *F. magellanica* and another species, *F.m.* 'Riccartonii' is the most planted, particularly as a hedging shrub. The growth is upright while the flowers, carried in generous quantities over many weeks, are particularly colourful – the corolla deep purple and the tube scarlet.

For twenty years I experimented with varieties which offered the prospect of being hardy. With most of the hybrids tried, good drainage frequently made the difference between a plant surviving or being killed by frost. Poor drainage is a curse and abomination to all the fuchsia clan; those not killed outright become pale reflections of similar plants grown on well drained soil. The garden where the fuchsias were grown lies 600 feet (180 m) above sea level in North Yorkshire and, though the trials were limited in scope, they were conclusive enough to convince me that many hardy varieties are ornamental plants not being employed to full advantage as permanent garden features.

'Alice Hoffman', with semi-double flowers, white in the corolla with a rose-pink tube and sepals, is neat and very compact. 'Corallina' introduced in 1845, and so one of the older hybrids now in cultivation, is excellent. I grew it trained to cover a south-facing potting shed, but it is seen to best effect as a free-growing shrub. The purple-tinged foliage is carried on elegantly arching stems. No variety flowers so profusely; the single blooms are scarlet and purple, and lovely when grown with deep blue lavender.

Another long-cultivated form, *F. magellanica globosa*, still holding a place if it came to me correctly named, made a compact, spreading shrub which was an excellent companion to the dark purple autumn-flowering *Crocus speciosus*. The flowers, which do not open to reflex as is usual, were like crimson and purple Chinese lanterns arranged along the stems. 'Genii' is an attractively foliaged very vigorous hybrid spreading in three years into a bush one yard (90 cm) across. The leaves, which are yellowish-green, set off the cerise and violet flowers to good advantage. This variety survived the hard winters of 1963 and 1981, but all top growth was cut to soil level.

Fuchsia 'Tom Thumb'

'Lena' spreads outwards rather than growing up, so it needs more space than most. Introduced in 1862, it has proved to be one of the toughest and most resilient. The semi-double blooms are flesh pink tinged with white, and with a mauve corolla. 'Margaret' is a most flamboyant 1949 introduction which reached 4 feet (1.2 m) high after a succession of mild winters; the semi-double corolla is violet in colour, the tube scarlet. Restricted to only one fuchsia, for good natured reliability after long association I would choose 'Mrs Popple', first grown in 1899. In most gardens it makes a shrub 4 feet (1.2 m) high. The tube of the flowers is a succulent soft crimson and the corolla violet, with the foliage a proper complement.

For the garden where space is at a premium there is a choice which includes 'Tom Thumb', 10 inches (25 cm) high, in carmine and purple, or a sport from this variety, also with semi-double flowers which are coloured light carmine and white. Where age takes precedence, then *F. magellanica* 'Pumila', 6 inches (15 cm) high and introduced in 1821, must be the choice with single flowers of bright red and mauve. Grown inter-

Right: *Fuchsia* 'Lena'
Far right: *Fuchsia* 'Mrs Popple'

mingled with the blue spikes of *Satureja montana* which is of similar height, dwarf fuchsias make a particularly pleasing composition.

Anyone fortunate enough to own a heated greenhouse will find the choice of varieties sufficient to satisfy the most selective gardener. The only certain way of making a selection is to visit a specialist show or nursery, or both. Fuchsias are capable of being trained into a variety of shapes which in their different ways show the beauty and quality of the flowers to best effect. This applies to plants grown in the garden or those cultivated in pots. Some form of pruning and training of the branch framework is essential to produce a well-flowered plant.

The bush form is the simplest, here the number of stems is restricted to what best suits the variety in hand. With some, three stems are sufficient, others will comfortably support six. Side shoots are stopped at two leaves, until the flowering framework is established.

The spherical or ball-head needs more attention. Only varieties which produce long-arching growth respond to this sort of training. By stopping shoots which form in the middle of the plant and training the outside branches to arch over and down, a very beautiful presentation is arrived at.

Standards and half standards are only possible with strong vigorous fuchsias, as the length of clean stem needed before the flowering head is formed can be anything from 18 to 42 inches (45 to 105 cm).

Espaliers and fan-trained forms are even more demanding of time and meticulous skill. For an espalier or fan the branch system is arranged so as to leave a short stem exposed for 2 or 3 inches (5 to 7 cm). The espalier is built up of branches trained out horizontally at intervals up the main stem. Ideally, these should be arranged opposite to each other on a flat plane left and right, but not all the way round.

The fan is, as the name implies, made up of a series of branches trained to form a triangular shape.

Varieties of fuchsia with lax or pendulous growth are best grown in hanging baskets. The most widely used for the purpose are 'Marinka', 'Golden Marinka', 'Cascade', and 'Falling Stars'.

To start a general collection, I would choose:

'Achievement' which, though a hundred years old, is easy to grow and train to most shapes. The flowers are cerise and purple.

'The Aristocrat', white, pink and pale rose is equal to any other in vigour and trainability.

'Aurora Superba', slim with 5 inch (12.5 cm) long flowers.

'Bon Accorde', again an old variety of stiff upright growth with purple and white flowers.

'Citation' makes good half-standards, rose pink and white.

'Dollar Princess', a real beginner's plant, cerise and purple.

'Glitter', long elegant flowers with delicate pink sepals and red tube.

'Lovable' because the colour combination is so lovely.

'Pink Jade', with delicate pink flowers.

'Snowcap' is an easily trained bush form with semi-double flowers in red and white.

'Swing Time', which responds to most styles and shaping, has double blooms coloured red and ivory white.

'Tennessee Waltz', a single rose-pink and lilac, made the best standard I have ever grown, with the least trouble.

'White Spider' with attractive white flowers. Ideal for a hanging basket or archway.

Golden foliaged varieties:

'Carl Drude' with red and white flowers.

'Gilda' golden green foliage, red and pink flowers.

Fuchsia 'Achievement'

Below left: *Fuchsia* 'Marinka'
Below: *Fuchsia* 'White Spider'

Top right: *Fuchsia* 'Falling Stars'
Right: *Fuchsia* 'Pink Jade'

Below: *Fuchsia* 'Swing Time'
Below right: *Fuchsia* 'Bon Accorde'

14
Peonies

The peony, according to ancient folk lore, drives away tempests and dispels enchantments, so in garden terms it is a plant both useful and beautiful. From early times the peony was held in high regard for its powers of healing. The name itself suggests this, being derived from Paeon, first physician of the Gods, who used peony root to cure Pluto of the wound inflicted on him by Hercules. In this country necklaces of beads made from peony root were worn by young children to help them in teething and as a protection against epileptic fits. The medicinal reputation is no longer acknowledged except in Chinese traditional medicine. Instead, the plant is valued on account of its ornamental flowers.

Until recently the genus *Paeonia* was placed in the same family as the buttercup, the Ranunculaceae. The flowers do show a similarity. Now it is separated from Ranunculaceae in a class of its own, the Paeoniaceae. Modern selections apart, the peony is an ancient plant in cultivation, particularly in terms of Chinese and Japanese gardening history.

Paeonia are mostly herbaceous perennials, apart from four species which develop a woody, shrub-like character, and are distinguished from the common herd by the popular name tree peony. *Paeonia delavayi* makes a deciduous shrub up to 6 feet (1.8 m) high, and is one of the hardiest. A handsome shrub with single flowers opening in May, the deep red petals are in bright contrast to the central cluster of yellow stamens. Seed is ripened most years, and this offers a simple way of raising fresh stock, if sown immediately the pod splits in the autumn. *P. delavayi* will grow in any reasonably fertile garden soil, and in every respect it is a most amiable shrub.

The plant was first discovered by the Abbé Delavay in the province of Yunnan in China, sometime during the ten years he was stationed at the mission there. Unfortunately, many of the boxes of plants which Delavay sent to Paris lay unopened for many years. So it was not until an English plant hunter, E. H. Wilson, sent seeds back to this country that *P. delavayi* was effectively brought under cultivation early in the present century. What is curious, is that Wilson had been sent out to China by the nursery firm of Veitch to collect the seeds of

Paeonia delavayi at the Royal
Botanic Garden, Kew

Davidia involucrata, the pocket handkerchief tree, and nothing else. The seeds of 305 different plant species, plus thirty-five cases of bulbs and live roots which Wilson also collected were merely incidental acquisitions which were to prove of immense benefit to gardeners.

The slightly dwarfer *P. lutea* was also discovered and, unlike *P. delavayi*, was actually introduced by the Abbé Delavay during his term in Yunnan about the year 1887. The flowers are 2½ inches (6 cm) across, slightly more in the better forms, with golden yellow petals. Indeed, in the variety *ludlowii* (introduced in 1936), which flowers earlier in May than the

Paeonia lutea ludlowii

type species, individual blooms can reach 5 inches (13 cm) in diameter. Growing as it does naturally at elevations of up to 11,000 feet (3300 m) *P. lutea* in all its forms is hardy in most gardens throughout the British Isles. Seed offers the best method of raising new plants.

The most important of the tree peonies is, undoubtedly, *P. suffruticosa* both in historical and garden terms. In wild plants the white-petalled, maroon or scarlet-centred blooms measure 6 inches (15 cm) across. The fragrance of these flowers, which open in May to June, is quite pleasant. The same cannot be said for some of the hybrids. A native of northern China, the moutan, *P. suffruticosa*, is now rarely found in a wild state. In Chinese gardens, however, the history of its cultivation goes back many centuries to when the first plants were introduced into the Imperial gardens during the seventh century AD. By the tenth century thirty-nine varieties were on sale. These varieties were propagated by grafting scions onto rootstocks of the wild species. 'Rock's Variety' is an attractive garden form with white petals and a large maroon blotch in the centre of the single or semi-double flowers.

The early introductions to Europe came from Canton, one of the areas visited by Robert Fortune, who was to make some interesting observations on the plants and people of China. Fortune noted that in Canton thousands of moutan peonies were imported each year from northern China. The popular Chinese name for the plant, moutan, roughly translated, means 'male vermilion'.

The moutan came to this country through the efforts of Sir Joseph Banks, who was keen to have specimens of such a

Paeonia lutea

Paeonia suffruticosa hybrid at
Walpole House Garden in London

Paeonia suffruticosa 'Rock's Variety'

desirable plant growing in Kew Gardens. He engaged a Mr Duncan who was in service with the East India Company to send plants to England. The first consignment arrived at Kew Gardens in 1787. Robert Fortune made his first expedition to China just over fifty years later, his plants went to the Horticultural Society's gardens, and proved to be hybrids with almost fully double flowers. Reginald Farrer, of alpine fame, was one of the fortunate few to have seen *P. suffruticosa* growing wild, in 1914 near Kaichow. Farrer waxed lyrical as only he could on 'the huge expanded goblets of Paeonia Moutan, refulgent as pure snow, and fragrant as heavenly roses'. Unfortunately, *P. suffruticosa* and its many cultivars is not predictably easy to grow. In the wild it enjoys complete winter dormancy, a resting period forced on it by quite severe frost and snow. This probably explains why the best specimens I know are growing in Yorkshire gardens where there is less danger of their being persuaded into precocious growth, only to have shoots and flower buds killed by late frost. A well-cultivated soil and a position facing north-west will suit the moutan. Annual mulching with rotted manure, leaf-mould or compost is a further subscription to ensure continued well-being of this lovely tree peony.

Propagation of the cultivars is usually by grafting onto either seedling *P. suffruticosa* or varieties of herbaceous peony.

How very easy it would be in considering the charms of tree peonies to overlook the qualities of the herbaceous species. In the final analysis they are more accommodating garden plants – they have lovely flowers, attractive foliage, and seed pods which in some species split open to reveal brightly-coloured seeds.

Paeonia mascula at Steep Holme

The first of the species known in this country was *P. mascula*, the male peony, arguably a native, more probably a feral monastry garden escape which grew wild near Winchcombe in the Cotswolds and Steep Holme in the Bristol Channel. A perennial between 18 and 24 inches (45 to 61 cm) high, with dark green leaves and deep red flowers 4 inches (10 cm) in diameter. There is a form from southern Europe and Asia Minor called *P. mascula arietina*. The plant I grew had leaves with a greyish down on the undersides, and beautiful cup-shaped flowers of rose-pink. *P. officinalis* is the female peony from the Mediterranean coast. I believe the names male and female are a legacy from the time when peonies were grown as medicinal plants. *P. mascula* or male peony was specific against disorders affecting men, *P. officinalis* or female peony was used for women's ailments.

Certainly, in 1548 *P. officinalis* was described by gardening writers of the time as common throughout England, presumably in gardens and not as a wild plant, either natural or feral. Hybrids derived from this species include some of the oldest and best loved of garden peonies. The old double-red 'Rubra Plena' is a particular favourite of mine, for it was the first of the clan of which I was aware. 'Rosea Superba Plena' is of a light-pink shade. Amongst the singles, 18 inch (45 cm) high 'China Rose', with cupped salmon-pink petals opening to reveal orange stamens, would be hard to improve on.

There is a surprisingly large number of plants which to all intents and purposes have become accepted through long association as British; *P. lactiflora* is one. Though this species was brought to this country two hundred years ago from Siberia, the Chinese had been growing and admiring it for a thousand years before that. The first importation died, so Sir Joseph Banks procured fresh stock from China early in the nineteenth century. This species is parent to many of the brightly coloured, sweetly fragrant Chinese peonies brought from China in those times. Another fifty years were to pass before James Kelway raised the hybridisation of peonies to new

Paeonia mascula arietina

Above: *Paeonia officinalis* at Kew
Right: *Paeonia lactiflora* 'Superba'

Paeonia mlokosewitschii

levels, producing a whole range of home-grown cultivars.

A native of Siberia, Mongolia, and northern China, *P. lactiflora* was valued as a medicinal plant. The Mongols made a soup of the roots, and used the powdered seeds to flavour tea.

There are many cultivars which owe at least some characteristic to *P. lactiflora*: 'Whitleyi Major' and 'The Bride' are two, with white, sweetly-scented flowers. Others include 'Superba', single off-white petals cupping yellow stamens; 'Sarah Bernhardt', double rose-purple petals edged with pink; and 'La France', single and semi-double rich rose-pink. In the type species, however, the flowers are white and sweetly-scented; they measure 4 inches (10 cm) across and are carried on 18-inch (45-cm) high stems during early June.

Any good garden soil that is well-cultivated and fertile will suit these plants, usually referred to as Chinese peonies. The roots are best left undisturbed. Soil fertility can be maintained with a dressing of fertiliser in late winter, together with a mulch of rotted manure or compost.

P. emodi is tall, up to 3 feet (90 cm) in height, and is found growing wild in the Northern Provinces of India. The golden stamened, white-petalled flowers have a pleasing scent. In my experience *P. emodi* is happier in partial shade. The shrub roses provide just the right amount of protection in this respect.

Inevitably, amongst the clan there has to be one member favoured above all others and, in spite of the name, *P. mlokosewitschii* has top place with me. The name is easy to remember if anglicised to 'Mock the Witch's Eye'. A native of the Caucasus, this species was introduced quite recently – during the first decade of this century. Always the first of the genus *Paeonia* to flower, in May, it is beautiful in all parts. The broad grey-green leaves provide the loveliest complement to the large lemon-yellow flowers. Then, in the late summer, the seed capsule splits to add a further distinction with red and black seeds. Compared to the other species at only 15 to 18 inches (38 to 45 cm) high, 'Mock the Witch's Eye' is a dwarf, though like the other new plants is easily raised from seed.

Though *P. obovata* is a native of Siberia and China, it expresses a profound dislike of the bitter east winds which are such a familiar experience in spring. Only in the warmest, most sheltered corners will this very beautiful peony thrive. There, the grey-green, copper-tinted leaves arch over to reveal 18-inch (45-cm) high flower spikes which each support one pure white-petalled, golden-centred bloom. I have never seen the flower any other colour but white, so I can only offer Henry Ford's choice 'of any colour providing it is white'. The soil needs to be enriched with leaf-mould, and a mulch of the same material every spring will seduce *P. obovata* into an extended associa-tion. For a long time I have searched for the form with pale primrose-coloured blooms known as 'Willmottiae' which I saw growing in a Devon garden. Like the Holy Grail of the Cru-saders it continues to elude me. But one peony which did not elude me was *P. clusii*. I found it growing on a stony hillside in Crete last year. The solitary white flowers were a pure delight. Two others, less well known perhaps, which have their home in that particular part of the world are *P. parnassica* (southern Greece) and *P. mascula hellenica*, the latter's name matching its natural beauty.

P. peregrina which is in many ways a more robust scarlet-flowered version of *P. obovata* is, fortunately, more easily accommodated. The foliage is a pleasant vivid green rather than grey, while the flowers are an unashamedly self-assertive fiery scarlet. Of the various hybrids of this species which are readily obtainable, 'Fire King' and the orange-tinted 'Sunshine'

Left: *Paeonia clusii* on a Cretan mountainside
Top: *Paeonia parnassica* in Greece
Above: *Paeonia obovata*

Paeonia mascula hellenica on a Greek hillside

Top: *Paeonia tenuifolia*
Above: *Paeonia veitchii woodwardii* 'Alba'
Right: *Paeonia tenuifolia* (pink form)

Below: *Paeonia humilis*

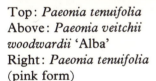

are good examples. In fertile, well-drained, heavy loam it reaches about 24 inches (60 cm) or slightly less on a soil which dries out rapidly under summer sunshine.

There are two species which would not be out of character when planted amongst dwarf shrubs on the outskirts of a large rock garden. *P. tenuifolia* is one, *P. veitchii* the other. *P. tenuifolia* is a Caucasian which was introduced to this country only forty years after *P. officinalis*, so it is no brash newcomer to our gardens. The leaves are so finely divided as to form a lacy Elizabethan ruff to the flowers. Of the two plants I have grown, both called *P. tenuifolia*, one had dark crimson, cup-shaped blooms, the other had deep pink. Both were equipped with a central boss of yellow stamens and grew no more than 16 inches (40 cm) high.

The second rock garden candidate *P. veitchii*, when satisfied with the accommodation offered, produces self-sown seedlings as an expression of gratitude. Only the largest, best coloured forms need be retained. Growing only 1 foot (30 cm) high, this neat Chinese species is, compared to *P. tenuifolia*, very much the new boy. It was brought to Britain during the first decade of the present century. A happy little plant with attractive mid-green leaves, and single, modestly nodding flowers which have petals of deep magenta. For those who find magenta unpleasant, the variety *P. veitchii woodwardii* 'Alba' offers an alternative. *P. humilis* is another low-growing species with red flowers and the attractive feature of dense hairs growing on the underside of the leaves.

P. cambessedesii is a slightly larger-growing plant, 18 inches (45 cm) in height. This has rose-pink flowers and the bonus of leaves which are deep green above and purple beneath. This peony does best against a wall or amongst shrubs.

My relationship with *P. wittmanniana* has been one of uneasy, grudging acceptance. The mistake happened early in our association when I grew it in close proximity to *P. mlokosewitschii*. Such comparisons on first acquaintance frequently lead to misunderstandings. *P. wittmanniana* has large leaves, shiny green on the upper surface and grey below. The white, lime-tinted flowers are large with a centre of red stamens. No sooner are they open to appreciation than the petals fall, and, apart from the scarlet and black of the open seed pods, the show is over for another twelve months. Given the company of blue-flowered *Brunnera* and *Polemonium*, it is a most attractive species so long as an overlong lunchbreak does not cause the proud gardener to miss the flowering time. The species was introduced from the north west Caucasus almost 150 years ago. Plants grown from seeds show variations in height from 20 up to 36 inches (50 to 90 cm), though this could have been caused by differences in soil fertility.

Early in the present century crosses were made between *P. lactiflora* and *P. wittmanniana*; 'Avant Garde' with peach-pink flowers is the best I have seen. None of the seedlings resulting from the cross set seed, a mule-like character which effectively restricts further experiments.

The crosses between *P. mlokosewitschii* and others have created nothing of real garden worth; the offspring I have seen were lacklustre – pink and white petals reminiscent of over-bleached laundry. Crosses between *P. lactiflora* and other European species offer profitable fields of exploration. No doubt in the course of time offspring from such crosses already in existence will be available to the gardening public at large.

Extensive crossing of many species has been carried out in the United States of America over the last fifty years. Some of

Paeonia cambessedesii

the hybrids are worth searching through catalogues to find – 'Constance Spry', a dark pink semi-double, 'Little Dorrit', salmon-red and compact in growth, and 'Moonrise', ivory-yellow, are three which should please and reward the diligent.

Interestingly enough, one cross between *P. mlokosewitschii* and *P. tenuifolia* produced something better than washed out laundry in 'Daystart', with a fine deep-yellow petal. This is a field of hybridisation open to anyone who grows peonies, whether amateur or professional. There is no better thrill of anticipation the garden affords than that of watching a colony of hybrid seedlings growing up to the first flush of flowers.

As a garden plant the peony makes little demand on the gardener's skill. Choose a sheltered place, particularly for the early flowering types, that is shaded from the early morning sun. This is to prevent buds caught by a late frost thawing out too quickly and being damaged. Before planting, it is well to prepare the soil thoroughly, as, given proper care, the roots should not need to be lifted for twenty years or more. Dig a dressing of rotted manure or compost into the bottom of the trench using a fork – so that the soil is loosened to a depth of 18 to 20 inches (45 to 50 cm). A dusting of complete fertiliser should be raked into the soil surface two weeks before planting. Extra phosphate encourages vigorous root development. When planted, the crown (buds) should sit just on the soil surface, no deeper than the level at which they were grown at the nursery.

Propagation of the species can be easily effected by sowing seed immediately it is ripe into a sandy compost. The containers can then stand outdoors, exposed to the frost. The only protection the seeds need is from mice who devour them avidly given the chance. Germination after winter stratification should take place the following spring.

The herbaceous hybrids can be divided just as growth starts in spring. Alternatively, lifting and division can be carried out in October. Replant straight away, so that the roots do not dry out.

Paeonia wittmanniana 'Avant Garde'

The various forms of tree peony, *P. suffruticosa* and others, apart from being grafted as previously described, can also be layered. Before growth begins in the spring, rake a dressing of sand and peat into the soil to bed the layer into. Use shoots of the previous year's growth, and make a cut between 4 to 6 inches (10 to 15 cm) from the tip, just deep enough to form a tongue 2 inches (5 cm) long. Peg the tongued branch firmly in place, then cover with the peat and sand compost. Rooting should have taken place well enough by the following spring for the layer to be potted up.

Rumours and paintings of Chinese origin suggest that yellow, green, and dark red tree peonies were grown there hundreds of years ago. Paintings in the Lindley Library support the theory that crosses had been made then between *P. lutea*, *P. delavayi*, and *P. suffruticosa*.

With modern propagation techniques all things are possible – and who knows what new brightly-coloured hybrids will grace our gardens in the years ahead.

15
Narcissus
(Daffodils)

There are some flowers which even the most determined non-gardener recognises immediately and greets with affection. Daffodils are one of the select band of universally popular plants. The name, so legend relates, derives from a handsome youth of Boeotia who, it was foretold, would live content unless and until he saw his own face. One day he stopped to slake his thirst in a pool, saw the reflection of his own beautiful features mirrored in the still water, and became so captivated he refused to be moved from the spot. Bewitched, he languished and died. Then, as Ovid relates, a flower sprang from the youth's corpse. Anyone who cares may look in the flower's cup and discover there the tears of Narcissus.

There is an interesting link between the poppy and Narcissus in the same legend. Pluto employed a flower of Narcissus to entice Ceres' daughter, Persephone, to the underworld. The poppy was created to enable the stricken Ceres to forget her grief in sleep. Other writers, less romantically inclined, say the name comes from the flower's narcotic qualities and its ability to dull the senses. That all the stories of a flower so pleasantly simple and beautiful are based on conceit or deceit is to do narcissus an unkindness. Shakespeare encompasses the character of all the lovely race in his *A Winter's Tale* – 'daffodils, That come before the swallow dares, and take The winds of March with beauty.' Poets other than Shakespeare praised the Lent lily and daffodowndilly, names which were formed from a still older title affodill, a corruption of *Asphodelus*, which now relates to an entirely different family.

Narcissi have been grown in gardens for close on four hundred years. Gerard lists a selection in his 1597 Herbal, while Parkinson in the early 1630s writes of seventy or eighty different kinds. Then for two hundred years interest in the development declined, a curious neglect which defies explanation. That the scent from the flowers was supposed to have a baneful influence causing headaches, melancholy, even insanity, may have limited the popularity of narcissi as decorative plants. This could be an exaggeration of pollen allergy; presumably there were people in those days who suffered from what is now described as hay fever, and some narcissus, par-

Narcissus pseudonarcissus captivated by its own reflection

Left: *Narcissus watieri*

ticularly the species *N. tazetta* and *N. jonquilla*, do have a very high perfume. Development of the flower in recent years more than makes up for the two centuries of neglect.

The greatest concentration of species occurring naturally is in the Mediterranean regions, Spain and Portugal being especially well endowed. Hybridisation occurs quite freely where the range of natural species overlaps, for example, *N. × medioluteus* (syn. *N. biflorus*) is suspected of being a natural hybrid of *N. poeticus × tazetta* by some authorities. Be that as it may, even without the bewildering variations in height, colour, shape, and flowering season which selective hybridisation has produced, the gardener who decides to grow species only will find these a fascinating field of exploration. From the tiny, delightful, though difficult to cultivate, *N. watieri* to the native *N. pseudonarcissus*, they welcome spring to our gardens alongside snowdrop and crocus.

Some species having been granted specific status have subsequently proved to be natural hybrids, but botanists still argue in quite heated terms on the subject. Fortunately, botanical precision is not part of the gardener's education, so when in doubt I consult the Royal Horticultural Society's Dictionary of Gardening for guidance, and then walk on tiptoe along the path the relevant page indicates.

N. asturiensis has been a garden friend and companion, tried and tested over many years. A tiny, deep yellow trumpet daffodil growing only 4 inches (10 cm) high which blooms early in the year, it is adventurously early in northern districts, and frequently suffers the punishment of weather-damaged flowers. That *N. asturiensis* grows under natural conditions some 6 to 7000 feet (1800 to 2100 m) up on mountain sides in northern Spain explains the bulbs' careless indifference to our weather. Given a sheltered corner of the rock garden which holds whatever warmth a pale February sun offers, this little species makes a lovely advance guard to the following legions.

Though all narcissus flowers share common characteristics except for modern hybrids, they do show considerable variation in size and shape of cup, as well as the petals (perianth segments in botanical terms). There is little of the obvious narcissus characteristic to be seen in the flowers of *N. bulbocodium* (hoop petticoat daffodil) to the casual eye. Certainly not in the strap-shaped, sometimes thread-like foliage, or in the curiously shaped flower. The long flaring trumpet, crinkled at the rim, and narrow petals give this variable species an elfin charm which is distinctive and attractive. There is a wide range of forms that vary from white to deep yellow. This variability occurs frequently in the wild, and this surprised me when I first saw the bulb growing under natural conditions. Native to south west France, north west Africa, Spain, and Portugal, it shows a catholic taste regarding soil type and situation. In the group I saw, some were growing in close-cropped turf near a rushing stream, others in shallow pockets of soil amongst large boulders. I suspect the rocks were limestone. There are many named varieties growing from 4 to 8 inches (10 to 20 cm) high,

Narcissus nobilis, like its near neighbour *Narcissus asturiensis*, grows wild in the mountainous regions of northern Spain

Below left:
Narcissus bulbocodium
Below:
Narcissus bulbocodium conspicuus

Right: *Narcissus* 'March Sunshine' growing with scillas

Narcissus bulbocodium mesatlanticus

some flowering in February, others delaying until early May. However, most bloom in April. The variety *N. bulbocodium citrinus* with flowers of primrose yellow is a native of north western Spain and is deservedly popular. *N. bulbocodium conspicuus* with deep yellow flowers is a strong-growing variety, but unless divided before the bulbs get overcrowded, it produces masses of leaves only. If planted in suitable soil under grass, both of these soon spread by seed and offsets into thriving colonies. Earliest of all to flower – usually in January, and therefore best grown in a cold greenhouse, *N. bulbocodium romieuxii* is a most desirable variety with pale yellow flowers. The Spanish and north African *N. cantabricus* is now a separate species, though it is so like *N. bulbocodium* that to the non-botanist they are of the same clan. As would be expected of any bulb from that area, they need a thorough sun-baking to succeed, so they are best grown in pots – well worth the trouble just to enjoy the delicate beauty unsullied by rain.

There is no mistaking the flowers of *N. cyclamineus* with their long trumpets and curious swept-back petals. A tough little species from Spain and Portugal, if given suitable soil conditions. I find the bulbs flourish in moist yet well-drained soil, spreading self-sown seedlings to fill all the available space. When grown naturalised the height is about 8 inches (20 cm), the flower colour, a rich gold. This species is, in truth, more notable for the numerous, excellent hybrids it has sired – 'Peeping Tom', 'February Gold', 'March Sunshine' and many more supply most useful spring bulbs where space is limited.

Though the modern varieties of trumpet daffodils are a result of crosses between various species, most of the yellow forms have the subspecies *N. pseudonarcissus major* (syn. *N. hispanicus*) as a parent. Originally located in southern France and Spain, the flowers are large, golden yellow and distilling a pleasant fragrance. The height is up to 24 inches (60 cm).

N. bicolor, parent of the two-toned trumpet narcissus, has similar large flowers having a corona of golden yellow and perianth segments of white or cream. The parentage of the white trumpet daffodils is shared between three or more species. The subspecies *N. pseudonarcissus moschatus* is a small flowered and modestly drooping plant. The sulphur and white flowers open from late April to May. Grown in a mass they have an unassertive charm, more so as the flowers are delicately fragrant.

Left and above:
Narcissus cyclamineus sheltering under *Rhododendron* × *praecox*

N. alpestris from the Pyrenees has the same modest
demeanour, and small flowers, pure white, are borne on six
inch (15 cm) stems. They open earlier than the other white
species in April. Of the other stud species, *N. albescens* with
off-white flowers, I know very little. It objected to the hospi-
tality offered, for after a frugal display of blossom in two years
it languished and died. Fortunately, this notable display of ill
manners has not been passed on to its offspring, which in a
fairly strong clay flourished exceedingly beyond all expectations.
Crossing between white, yellow, and bicolor species has produced the enormous range of colours on offer at the present
time. However, *N. alpestris* and *N. albescens* have been united
with *N. pseudonarcissus moschatus* by modern authors – (a
subspecies of great variation with a wide geographical distribution).

There is an understandable tendency to assume that all species of narcissus are hardy, adapting easily to garden conditions. While the majority do, there are some which only grow when given specialised cultivation. The jonquil, together with near relatives *N. rupicola* and *N. requienii* offer a challenge to the skill of those who attempt to grow them. The jonquil *N. jonquilla*, with rush-like leaves is one which continues to resist all my efforts. The yellow flowers carried on 10-inch (25-cm) stems are heavily perfumed. Grown in a cold greenhouse, they make a pleasant accompaniment to the alpines which also enjoy protection from inclement weather. *N. requienii*, a tiny member of the group which comes from northern Spain is a gem only 6 inches (15 cm) high. Up to five yellow flowers open on the stems, each one with a frilled central cup. Six bulbs maintain a precarious existence in the well-drained soil of a table bed. When I see the flowers which open in late March or early April being battered with heavy rain or sleet, I do feel that this fragile beauty would be happier in the greenhouse. Not so *N. rupicola*, which has made a bed half-way up a south-facing slope in the rock garden a home from home. It is hardly surprising that the bulbs thrive in stony ground, for in the wild they grow 6 to 7000 feet (1800 to 2100 m) up the mountain sides in Portugal. The flowers 1½ inches (3.5 cm) in diameter and deep yellow in colour are carried singly on 6-inch (15-cm) stems during May. Good drainage is absolutely essential or these bulbs will not flourish. *N. juncifolius* is another fine miniature jonquil.

Spain offers another daffodil of dwarf stature which fits neatly into the small garden landscape in *N. minor*. Growing about 8 inches (20 cm) high, the flowers in two tones of yellow are large in proportion to the stem length. I grew a form with full double flowers in my last garden which came to me as 'Queen Anne's Daffodil'.

Should I ever be asked to propose an archetype daffodil, then my choice would fall on *N. pseudonarcissus* which is naturalised in so many places throughout the British Isles. There are many different forms, usually with white petals and

Top: *Narcissus jonquilla*
Above: *Narcissus juncifolius*
Below left: *Narcissus minor*
Below: *Narcissus pseudonarcissus*

lemon yellow trumpets with an average stem length of 12 inches (30 cm). The largest concentration of this species I have ever seen occurs in Farndale, Yorkshire, where the bulbs have established over many acres in the damp fields – conditions much to this daffodil's liking. The picture they make when in bloom on a sunlit April day remains vivid in the memory. At one period this species formed a convenient dumping ground for any trumpet daffodils which needed classification, including the Tenby daffodil, *N. obvallaris* with self-coloured, yellow flowers. Certainly the two are very closely related, though the Tenby daffodil lacks the robust constitution of the typical form.

There are two pheasant's eye narcissi. *N. poeticus* and the, so-called, old pheasant's eye variety, *N. poeticus recurvus* – the popular name is misleading in that the latter was introduced from Switzerland only a hundred years ago, much later than *N. poeticus*. *N. poeticus* flowers are white-petalled with a red cup, as found wild in the mountain areas of central and southern Europe. There must be many different forms, for the flowering season extended in my last garden from April until early June. *N. poeticus recurvus* has white-petalled flowers whose chrome yellow cup is edged with scarlet.

All the pheasant's eye types are scented and pleasantly so. I like to see them naturalised under apple trees in a grassed-down orchard – with the play of sunlight filtering through the branches overhead making a patina across the flowers, or growing wild, as I so frequently found them, in moist alpine meadows against the commanding landscape of the mountain above La Grave.

Of all the genus the little cup or bunch-flowered narcissus, *N. tazetta* is the most cosmopolitan. Its range extends from Syria through Kashmir to China. Paintings offer a record that this narcissus was grown in China one thousand years ago. There it is persuaded to grow in time for the Chinese new year, hence the popular name new year lily. The Tazettae section of narcissus is not easy to establish in gardens, except those with a very favourable climate, though some of the varieties bred from

Above: *Narcissus poeticus hellenicus*
Below: *Narcissus obvallaris*
Below right:
Narcissus tazetta pachybolbos

species are of stronger constitution. By the early part of the nineteenth century there were about three hundred varieties being grown by Dutch nurserymen. A species of the Tazettae section, which has become naturalised on the Scilly Isles, occasioned a change in the islands' farming economy and practice. Boxes of naturalised 'Scilly Whites' which were picked and sent as a speculation to market by a local farmer proved so profitable that it encouraged him to include cultivating narcissus as part of his crop rotation. The practice spread amongst the islands' farmers until exporting cut blooms became a major source of income.

It is a pity that the Tazettae section are not truly hardy, as the cluster-headed, sweetly-scented flowers appearing as they do so early in the year would be a most welcome addition to the garden scene. They are, however, excellent for forcing under glass; cultivated varieties such as 'Paper White' (*N. papyraceus*) and lovely 'Soleil d'Or' make a brave show in mid-winter, given just a modest amount of heat. Reports on how the narcissus was introduced to the Scillies are contradictory. The most romantic is that of a ship carrying bulbs as a cargo being wrecked on the shore – whether the bulbs were washed up on the beach or were taken ashore by looters is not clear. In fact, the suggestion that Benedictine monks carried bulbs with them from Spain when they established a cell on the island has more validity.

A cross-pollination made late in the nineteenth century by a firm of Dutch bulb growers between *N. poeticus* (pheasant's eye) and *N. tazetta* resulted in hybrids which flower later and are hardier than *N. tazetta* – known as *N. × poetaz*. One of the best known of the hybrids, 'Geranium' carries up to six pure white flowers per stem, each with an orange-scarlet centre.

Comparisons are easily made in some things, never between flowers do they have any great deal of meaning, yet in company with the majority of gardeners when *N. triandrus* is in flower I do feel this is, perhaps, the loveliest of all the species. As would be expected with any bulb which inhabits the north Spanish mountains, *N. triandrus albus* adapts to the cool climate of

Narcissus 'Paper White'

Narcissus triandus concolor

these islands more readily than the species from the hot sun-baked Mediterranean. In my experience the flowers last for several weeks when the bulbs are planted in shade, even seeding themselves if the bulbs are left undisturbed. I have never seen the true species except in the wild, as the bulbs sent as *N. triandrus* have always proved to be hybrids. All have greyish green rounded leaves and pendant flowers with reflexing petals. *N. triandus albus*, commonly known as the angel's tears narcissus, are white. Deep yellow-flowered forms are found in the subspecies *N. triandus concolor* and *N. triandus aurantiacus* from northern Portugal. In spite of never having acquired the true species, I find the nodding, pensive charm of *N. triandus* cultivated varieties irresistible. All of them flower during April in my garden.

I expressed the opinion previously in this chapter that *N. watieri*, a tiny jonquil, was not easy to grow and it does, in most cases, warrant that reputation. I grew six bulbs for something over ten years in a well-drained bed amongst heathers. There, this beautiful little species opened solitary, pure white flowers on 4- to 6-inch (10- to 15-cm) high stems. No doubt the heathers sucked up excess moisture, and the bulbs ripened fully as a result. Conditions identical with those which bulbs growing in the wild enjoy on steep Moroccan mountain slopes.

The choice of what species or cultivar to grow depends on the facilities the garden can offer for their accommodation. In an alpine lawn, or amongst dwarf shrubs, or ledges in the rock garden, *N. cyclamineus*, *N. minor*, *N. rupicola*, *N. bulbocodium* and cultivars derived from them will be most suitable. For naturalising, the taller *N. poeticus*, *N. pseudonarcissus*, and the stronger-growing, more vigorous hybrids are to be preferred. To provide a spring bedding, or in groups down the border, great play can be made with the brighter-petalled modern hybrids.

Narcissi thrive best in a strong, fertile, well-drained soil. They do not appreciate being planted in soil dressed with fresh farmyard manure, as I discovered to my cost some years ago. Once established, the flowering of the bulbs will be improved by an annual feed with a complete fertilizer at 2 oz (56 g) per square yard, each year in February. Bulbs are best planted in August, if possible, so that the roots are well established by the time growth stops at the onset of cold weather.

Depth of planting depends on the bulb size: smaller species 2 to 3 inches (5 to 8 cm) deep, larger-flowered species and hybrids 4 to 6 inches (10 to 15 cm) deep in bare soil, 6 to 8 inches (15 to 20 cm) deep in grassed-down land. Experiments have shown that if the foliage is left for six weeks from when the flowers fade, it can then be cut without appreciably harming the next season's blossoming. With the more temperamental species I err on the side of caution by letting the foliage wither away naturally. Narcissi are such a lovely embellishment to the spring scene that they are worth a place in the most selective gardens. That they are so widely planted is a compliment to their popularity.

16
Delphiniums

Considering that there are few plants which have contributed more to the beauty of our gardens than delphiniums, there is very little information about the origins of hybrid forms. There are upward of two hundred species, some are perennial, others biennial, while the remainder including the popular larkspur are annual. The species grow wild in North America, Europe, Asia, North Africa, and one province of China – namely Szechwan. Though three species are listed as wild plants in the British Isles, all are considered to have been introduced, even the forking larkspur, *Delphinium consolida*.

Herbalists were well acquainted with the delphinium's poisonous properties, the active principle delphinia was said to act on the nervous system. Delphinium seeds were used as a powerful purgative, as a cure for toothache, and, when mixed as a salve, to treat skin diseases. The main value of the powdered seed was its ability to destroy lice on both humans and animals, hence the popular name lousewort.

The name *Delphinium* derives from the Greek word *delphis* – a dolphin. The shape of the flower-bud, particularly that of the annual species, suggested a comparison to a leaping dolphin. Though the plants, initially, enjoyed consideration more for

Delphinium consolida

The author admiring the delphiniums at 'The Heath' near Leeds

their medicinal values than as garden decoration, for such a distinctive specimen as the delphinium there is, indeed, little more than casual reference. In the late sixteenth century note is made of a species, *D. staphisagria*, growing 2 to 3 feet (60 to 90 cm) high with flowers blue and white. This was grown, if records are correct, only in Italian gardens for medicinal purposes, and is not important in plant breeding. On the other hand *D. consolida* enjoys a somewhat better press. Once the common larkspur of gardens, this is an attractive European annual 30 inches (75 cm) high with violet or blue flowers. Records in the sixteenth century relate that it was valued as a herb for dressing wounds. Indeed, the name *consolida* – to make firm – confirms this. An infusion of the herb in water was recommended as a cure for eye complaints.

Medicinal virtues apart, the introduction of another annual, *D. ajacis*, rocket larkspur, from the Mediterranean region provided scope for the hybridist, and it is largely from this species, rather than the common larkspur, that the popular annuals so widely grown in gardens today have been developed. There is, it seems, some disagreement as to which species, *D. ajacis* or *D. consolida*, has priority – no doubt, the argument will resolve itself. Growing anything from 1 to 3 feet (30 to 90 cm) high, with double or single flowers, ranging in colour from blue, lavender, rose, pink, and white, hybrid larkspurs are easily grown in most soils as hardy annuals.

Seed is best sown directly where the plants are to flower, in April or early May. I have sown seed under cloches in September to provide early spikes of bloom for indoor decoration. Curiously, within a few years of the introduction of this species late in the sixteenth century, writers of that period were describing it as a weed in cornfields – which speaks well for adaptability if nothing else.

According to some authorities, the first truly perennial delphinium to arrive in this country was brought from the Pyrenees. Mongolia is given as the source by others. In writings on things horticultural about 1640, mention is made of both single and double forms. Described as a strong-growing perennial of up to 6 feet (1.8 m) high, with pale blue-violet flowers, *D. elatum* is considered to be the primary ancestor of popular hybrids like 'Swanlake' and 'Daily Express' grown in gardens today. Most writers on the subject agree to *D. elatum* as one parent, while suggesting by reasoned argument that the other species used in the hybridisation of delphiniums, as grown in modern gardens, are the result of work done initially by the nursery firm of Kelways which began specialist breeding of delphiniums in the mid 1800s. Fifty years or so later Blackmore and Langdon, whose name is now virtually synonymous

Right:
Delphinium 'Daily Express' with *Geranium armenum* 'Bressingham Flair' in the foreground

Prize delphiniums growing in Blackmore and Langdon's Nursery near Bristol

with delphiniums, also took an interest in the subject. American breeders, stimulated by the expressed interest from gardeners in the United States, also began experimental hybridisation, producing several fine varieties with fragrant flowers in the process.

How the smaller, repeat-flowering Belladonna hybrids like 'La Maritime' were generated is not known for certain. If looks are a guide, the neatly compact and pretty *D. grandiflorum* may lay some claim to parentage. In my experience, neither the species *D. grandiflorum*, nor the hybrids derived from it – 'Blue Bees', 'Butterfly', 'Peace', or 'Azure Fairy' are long-lived perennials, unless kept going by propagating new stock. They are, however, lovely to look at and well worth a little extra trouble even though no birth certificate is available. In certain circumstances I have sown seed of the species in April and had the resulting plants flowering in late July. There is a species closely related to *D. grandiflorum* which originates in the

Above left: *Delphinium* 'Swanlake'
Above right: An unnamed Belladonna
seedling in California

Left: *Delphinium* 'La Maritime'
Right: *Delphinium* 'Blue Bees'
Far right: *Delphinium grandiflorum*

Left: *Delphinium tatsienense*
Above: *Delphinium nudicaule*

Below and right:
Delphinium cardinale in a
Californian hedgerow

Szechwan province of China – *D. tatsienense* by name. Over the years I have grown dozens of this dwarf delphinium from seed for planting in small borders or in a rock garden. The leaves are finely divided, the violet-blue flowers with cream centre appear in mid-summer. In a sheltered, well-drained bed this species makes a good short-lived perennial. Another species suited to rock garden cultivation is *D. luteum* from California. This has attractive cream-yellow flowers and stands 12 to 18 inches (30 to 45 cm) high.

Amongst a genus with predominantly blue flowers, the appearance of two delphiniums, *D. nudicaule*, and *D. cardinale* with red-petalled blooms, is a refreshing piece of individualism. I have only grown *D. cardinale* as an annual, for the very simple reason that none of the seedlings survived the winter. It is not surprising that neither of the red-flowered species accept our climate, being natives of California. In the southern regions of that sunshine state I found *D. cardinale* growing up through poison oak on a sun-baked hillside. It grows in almost pure state, and the scenery forms a dramatic backcloth for a most

Left and above:
Dr Legro's University hybrids

spectacular species. *D. nudicaule* is a pygmy, growing only 10 inches (25 cm) high with flower spikes of orange-red. The shades vary – some are better than others. Given shelter and good drainage *D. nudicaule* should be capable of surviving the winter outdoors in the maritime gardens. A hybrid between *D. nudicaule* and an unknown garden delphinium was achieved in the late 1920s after many attempts by a Dutch nurseryman. Only one seedling showed hybrid characteristics. The second generation of seedlings were of the Belladonna character with pink flowers, marketed under the cultivar name 'Pink Sensation'. In a mild climate, with good cultivation in the form of a well-prepared, freely draining soil, 'Pink Sensation' will prove a moderately sound perennial. Those, like myself, who are conditioned to mistrust our climate, will keep a stock plant indoors just in case. The height varies appreciably between 30 inches and 48 inches (0.9 and 1.2 m). It is a delightfully formed little delphinium for those who are prepared to make the effort needed to grow it successfully.

Two other species are of importance, not in their value as garden plants, but rather as tools in the hands of hybridists. *D. wellbyi* from Abyssinia with greenish-blue fragrant flowers is not sufficiently hardy to be grown outdoors. The species is being used tentatively to try and introduce a quality notably lacking in delphiniums generally – namely scented flowers. *D. zalil* from Persia is another tender importation with pale yellow flowers. Crossing between the species is not easy, requiring skill and patience, as quite often seedlings from the inter-pollination have proved sterile. The man who for many years has been conducting experiments in breeding delphiniums is Dr R. A. Legro, who began work in the University of Wagenin-

Delphinium 'Blue Tit'

gen in Holland thirty years ago, and has continued at the Royal Horticultural Society's garden at Wisley. He has used the species *D. zalil* with the red-flowered *D. nudicaule* and *D. cardinale*. The aim of Dr Legro was to breed hardy border delphiniums with large spikes of yellow, red, and orange flowers to complement those with the blue or white flowers normally available in commerce. To a degree this has been successful, although the limited number of the pink and fawn-coloured varieties I have tried lack the robust constitution of established *D. elatum* cultivars. Grown on strong clay soil, they showed a lessened resistance to fungal infection. Though I understand that varieties are now available which are sound perennials of robust constitution, it will be a major landmark in garden history to have delphiniums combining pink, yellow, or blue flowers with fragrance. To share the popularity of *D. elatum*, they must be adaptable to a wide range of soils, climatic conditions, and be easily increased by means of cuttings.

Work done in America during the 1950–70s resulted in the Pacific hybrid strain of delphiniums which grow from seed to flower very quickly. Under our climatic conditions they are better grown as annuals or biennials. They show a wide range of flower colour including with the normal blue and purple, shades of pink, fawn, and white. Seed sown under glass in March will provide the garden with a display of blossom during August and September which extends the delphinium's season considerably. Treated as biennials, Pacific hybrids flower in late May giving spikes of fine quality.

The even more recent strains of dwarf delphiniums which are available, and can be easily raised from seed, make a very lovely addition to the range. Those I have grown, namely 'Blue Tit' and 'Blue Jade', produced spikes of flowers 30 to 36 inches (75 to 90 cm) high. 'Blue Tit' are mostly double-flowered in indigo-blue with a small black-brown eye. 'Blue Jade' has

Delphinium 'Blue Jade'

Left: *Delphinium* 'Butterball'
Centre: *Delphinium* 'Strawberry Fair'
at the Royal Horticultural Society's
Garden at Wisley

blooms of a pale sky blue made even more vibrant by the contrasting brown eye in the centre. Taller varieties, up to 9 feet (2.7 m) high, which I have successfully grown include 'Butterball', a rich cream colour with a yellow eye; 'Strawberry Fair', a purple-rose with a white eye; and 'Fanfare', an attractive mauve with a white eye.

New techniques in plant breeding will, I am sure, see an ever-increasing variation in the quality and range of delphiniums. In California new dwarf delphiniums have been bred which are only 18 inches to 3 feet (45 to 90 cm) high. All the plants I saw growing had good, well-formed flower spikes in almost every shade of blue, and recent developments have produced plants with white flower spikes. This surely must be an advantage for the smaller garden, with no need for staking being an added bonus. In general, delphiniums are not hard to grow so long as basic requirements of soil and shelter are met. They need a soil which is deep, well-drained and fertile. The plants die back to soil level, so each year they have to make an enormous amount of new growth, then yield a flower spike – a feat only possible if the roots are in a rich soil. Anyone who has lifted five-year-old delphiniums and seen the amount of root development will appreciate just how deep delving they are.

The ideal site would be in the open, exposed to all the sunshine available, yet sheltered from strong winds. To prepare the soil whether it is heavy clay, light sand, or all grades between, trench dig the bed in the autumn prior to spring planting. Though it may sound laborious, make certain this initial preparation is thorough. After opening up a 20-inch (50-cm) wide trench, lay manure, compost, or whatever organic matter is available in the bottom. Fork along the trench bottom breaking up any hard-panned soil and mix in the organic material. This should give a working depth of 20 inches (50 cm) or so, well-drained in winter yet moisture retentive in summer. Plenty of moisture is important as the delphinium makes virtu-

Right: *Delphinium* 'Fanfare'

ally all its growth in April, May and June when rainfall is spasmodic. In the late winter when the soil has settled give the bed a dressing of lime. A simple pH test will give a rough guide as to how heavy the application should be. Delphiniums, like most herbaceous plants find a neutral soil most acceptable. Lime improves the structure of clay soil, releases certain essential minerals, and neutralises acids.

Planting up the bed can be carried out towards the end of April. Delphinium species and cultivars are easily raised from seed providing it is harvested and sown quickly. Alternatively the seed can be harvested, cleaned, then stored in a cool temperature of 34 to 38°F. (1 to 3°C.) until sowing time. Delphinium seed loses viability, but cool storage conditions prevent this happening. Though the seed can be sown directly where the plants are to flower, the gardener has more control over germination if the work is done in a frame or greenhouse. Either peat- or loam-based compost can be used, but in practical terms John Innes seed compost has proved most reliable over the twenty years or more I have grown delphiniums. A high temperature is not essential for germination – 55 to 60°F. (12 to 16°C.) is quite adequate. Higher temperatures and humidity increases the risk of seedlings damping off. The seedlings of both annual and perennial species are pricked off when large enough to handle. Annuals will do well in seed boxes; perennials suffer root disturbance at planting-out time unless they are grown on in pots. Once again, the peat- or loam-based mixtures are suitable, though if seed was grown in one or the other the young plants should be kept on the same diet. My seedlings go from John Innes seed compost to the No. 1 potting mixture. Just prior to planting, about 2 weeks beforehand, dress the plot with 2 oz (56 g) per square yard of complete fertilizer.

Established plants already growing in the garden are best increased by means of basal cuttings, made from young shoots which push up from the root crowns in early spring. Some shoot-thinning on delphiniums is essential, for, if all are left to develop, the flower spikes will be of poor quality and overcrowded. Sever the cuttings close to the rootstock, then dibble them either into pots or a cold frame filled with a compost of 2 parts sharp sand and 1 part peat. Cuttings which show black marks or hollow stems are best discarded. Shoots 4 inches (10 cm) long, slightly thicker than a pencil, offer good cutting material. In my experience no extra heat is needed to help the cuttings to root – the cool and slow technique makes the sturdiest plants. Usually rooting takes place in 4–5 weeks, and the cuttings are ready for potting off into 3-inch (7-cm) pots filled with John Innes No 2. compost. Cuttings taken in early April should be ready for planting in their flowering positions by July.

Though the progressive improvement in both the quality and colour of flowers is largely a result of specialist skill assisted by modern science, anyone can make crosses which will create an interesting crop of seedlings. Usually the lower florets which open first are selected for pollination. Choose a spike to be the seed parent then, just as the flowers start to open, remove the petals (eye or bee petals) which protect the anthers and ovaries. Using a pair of tweezers remove the anthers very carefully – this emasculates the floret so preventing self-pollination. At

Above: A field in California of *Delphinium* 'Blue Springs', a dwarf variety

Delphinium 'Snowdon'

this stage the ovaries are very small and hard to see, and great care must be exercised to ensure they are not damaged. The pollen from the plant selected as the male parent is transferred to the stigma of the prepared floret immediately it is sufficiently mature. This is indicated when the tip of the stigma secretes a sticky substance, which holds the pollen grains firmly. After pollination is completed enclose the treated floret in a muslin bag to prevent unscheduled, extra pollination by insects. As the seed capsule swells it is advisable, though not essential, to strip all the other florets from the stem as the petals fade. This concentrates the plant's energy on the legitimate seed, instead of wasting it unnecessarily on capsules which are eventually going onto the compost heap.

Raising a healthy batch of young delphinium seedlings from your own selected parents and watching them coming into flower for the first time is both exciting and rewarding. But if you want to see how the experts fare, then visit the trials field in the Royal Horticultural Society's garden at Wisley where the best plants are selected and subsequently given awards. In 1983 some of the best were D. 'Corinth' (which received an Award of Merit), and D. 'Emily Hawkins' and D. 'Snowdon' (both gaining First Class Certificates).

Delphinium 'Emily Hawkins'

17
Dianthus and Carnations

What's in a name? A great deal when applied to some plants; and surely, Theophrastus writing in 300 BC must have been poetically inspired when choosing the name for *Dianthus*. Divine flower, blossom of Jove or Zeus, whichever translation that learned writer intended, each aptly describes a plant whose popularity continues undiminished over the passage of centuries. The genus is a large one of over three hundred species, including members which are better known by their popular names – sweet William, carnation, and pink.

So often, flowers which delighted the embryo gardener are discarded as other plants are introduced and experience ripens in maturity. Some, such as the dianthus, survive the test of time to become an essential part of the pattern. Both carnations and pinks have been cultivated in gardens for so long that the early stages of development which resulted in the flowers grown today are not recorded.

Our own native *Dianthus armeria*, the Deptford pink, which is a biennial, gives a fair indication of what the ideal conditions are for the family. Now somewhat of a rarity, it can still be found on sandy, dry pastures. So without exception, dianthus prefer a well-drained soil and a place in full sun. Even so, to maintain healthy, well-flowered specimens it is essential to keep rejuvenating them by raising fresh stock from cuttings.

Dianthus armeria

Dianthus 'Frances Isobel'

Fortunately, young growths pulled off the parent plant in late summer will root readily when inserted into a sandy compost. Seed offers an alternative method of increasing stock of the species, and can be sown immediately it is ripe, or in April at the start of the growing season. A loam- or peat-based compost will give an adequate germination, though I have a personal preference for the John Innes seed mixture when sowing pink or carnation seed.

The carnation is supposed to have obtained its name from the flesh-coloured flowers, yet early writers refer to the flowers as coronations. The name gilliflower is easier to discover, being a corruption of the Latin specific name *carvophyllus*, a clove. This is a reference to the spicy odour of the

flowers which were used as a substitute for the expensive Indian cloves, much sought after as a flavouring in the preparation of certain dishes. Clove pinks were highly commended by herbalists as a treatment for nervous disorders, and to induce perspiration in those suffering from typhus and other fevers.

The carnation is derived from the species *Dianthus caryophyllus* which, according to the Royal Horticultural Society's Dictionary of Gardening, varies little in nature, though a great deal under cultivation. Several different forms do, however, occur in the Atlas Mountains, which tends to confirm Pliny's opinion expressed two thousand years ago that it is of Spanish origin. Certainly, legend has it that the carnation was brought to this country by the Normans and that the Moors were growing double carnations in the thirteenth century. It is said that it was these, when introduced to Europe from Tunis, which made them such a popular garden flower. The species *D. caryophyllus* has a deep-pink flower, so other species must have been used to procure the many and various shades available at the present time. Possibly *D. knappii* with a nondescript yellow flower may have played a part. In the sixteenth century double dianthus were illustrated in Persian pottery and tiles. The petals of these early hybrids usually show stripes or splashes of a different colour tone. Variously known as picotees and bizarres, it is not recorded whether they resulted from contrived cross-pollination or as a result of selection from random crosses.

In the middle of the eighteenth century a repeat blooming

Dianthus 'George Woodfield'

Dianthus 'Fragrant Ann'

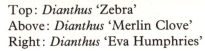
Top: *Dianthus* 'Zebra'
Above: *Dianthus* 'Merlin Clove'
Right: *Dianthus* 'Eva Humphries'

carnation, which flowered from June until September, was raised in southern France. At about the same time carnations were being suggested more as a pot plant for the greenhouse than as a perennial to be grown in the open garden. The nineteenth century saw the introduction of perpetual 'Malmaison' and 'Chabauds' strains. Even under glass and with the modern aids to cultivation enjoyed today, it takes skill to grow perpetual and Malmaison carnations well. How the perpetual carnation was achieved is not known for certain. One suggestion which seems the most credible is that it is a hybrid between *D. caryophyllus* and the Chinese or Indian pink, *D. chinensis*, an annual or sometimes biennial species with pink or white flowers flecked and spotted with dark red. So once again it is a union between east and west which, as with roses, has been responsible for introducing a popular perennial to garden cultivation.

The breeding of perpetual carnations was for many years confined to France and America. 'Mrs Thomas W. Lawson', a cerise-pink, and 'Victor Emmanuel', crimson and scarlet on yellow, were two important stud varieties – parents of a whole new generation of florists' perpetual carnations. The British contribution, with cultivars 'Winter Cheer' crossed earlier this century with 'Mrs Thomas W. Lawson', gave 'Britannia' – a delightful non-fading scarlet-flowered form. Nowadays, varieties such as 'Fragrant Ann', white, 'George Woodfield', cream, edged with crimson, and 'Joanne', deep cerise, are among the showmen's favourites.

As the parent of border and perpetual carnations with their brightly coloured, sweetly-scented flowers, *D. caryophyllus* is a classic example of floral development at the hands of gardener hybridists.

Border carnations should be planted in a sunny position into a soil which is well drained. Prepare the site by digging in a light dressing of well-rotted compost or farmyard manure, burying it about 8 to 10 inches (20 to 25 cm) deep. On heavier soil a bed raised about 6 inches (15 cm) above the general level will make sure of good drainage, essential if the plants are to thrive. The young stock is planted 15 to 18 inches (38 to 45 cm) apart in April. Reliable varieties include 'Eva Humphries' – white ground picotee with dark red edging, 'Merlin Clove' – white, marked with crimson, 'Zebra' – yellow, marked with crimson, and 'Harmony' – grey-flecked cerise.

Annual carnations require similar soil conditions and spacing. Most varieties will grow between 2 to 3 feet (60 to 90 cm) high, so some form of support is necessary. The carnation hoops made from heavy gauge galvanised wire serve the purpose best, and are inconspicuous as well. To ensure good quality blooms, as the flower stems develop remove all buds except those at the tips of the shoots. A feed of bone meal or similar organic fertiliser applied each year in spring will maintain the soil fertility. 'Fire Carpet', Chabaud and 'Queens Court' are recommended strains.

The cultivation of perpetual flowering carnations in a greenhouse is both interesting and rewarding. Given good light in a well-ventilated atmosphere, with a winter temperature of 45–50°F. (7–10°C.) minimum the carnation will produce good crops of flowers. The young cuttings should be grown in John Innes No 1 compost in a pot no larger than 3½ inches (9 cm) to begin with. When large enough, transfer to 6 inch (15 cm) pots

Below left: *Dianthus* 'Queens Court'
Below: *Dianthus* 'Vera Woodfield'

Dianthus plumarius

Dianthus 'Sussex Fortune'

filled with John Innes No 2 compost. Pinch out the growing tip when ten pairs of leaves have formed. This will encourage side shoots to grow, and these should be stopped at five leaves. How many more stops are made depends on when the plants are required to flower – two stops will mean an autumn crop. As the flower buds develop give a feed – either dry or liquid at ten day intervals. Remove all buds except the crown bud at the top. Top show varieties include 'Sussex Fortune' – brilliant scarlet, striped crimson, 'Boltonian' – crimson, and 'Vera Woodfield' – pale yellow.

Cuttings made from non-flowering side shoots, taken in winter and inserted in sharp sand over bottom heat, will root in four to six weeks. Seed is an alternative method of propagation, and often creates interesting colour forms. It can be sown into pots filled with seed compost in February to March.

Garden pinks enjoy a wider acclaim than the carnation, possibly because they need less specialised cultivation. Though several species are thought to have contributed, the main parent is *D. plumarius* which grows in lime-rich soil and in the mountainous terrain of south-western Europe. The fragrant, fringe-petalled flowers on 4- to 12-inch (10- to 30-cm) high stems are pink. In natural conditions, forms with white and deeper pink flowers with a central blotch have been recorded. These offered early hybridists material to work with and select from.

Our own native Cheddar pink, *D. gratianopolitanus*, also with fringed pink-petalled flowers is one species almost

Top left: *Dianthus* 'Diane'
Below left: *Dianthus* 'Mrs Sinkins'

Top: *Dianthus* 'Laced Monarch'
Centre: *Dianthus* 'Doris'
Below: *Dianthus* 'Ruby Doris'

certainly used for cross-pollination with *D. plumarius*. Laced pinks which were a favourite of the Paisley weavers own the same ancestry as the well-known *D. × allwoodii* and were obtained by crossing border carnations with established varieties of garden pink. So in reality, though *D. plumarius* is the prime progenitor, the Cheddar pink, Chinese pink, and carnation all assisted at one stage or another in creating the garden pink.

The hybrids are grouped in colours as selfs or single coloured; bicolours – with two distinct shades; laced – where the petals are edged with the same shade as that of the central blotch; and fancies where the petals are flecked with irregular markings.

Garden pinks grow from 10 to 15 inches (25 to 38 cm) high and have grey-green leaves with single or double flowers, usually appearing in June to July. Good old varieties include 'Mrs Sinkins' – white petalled and very fragrant, 'Inchmery' – pale pink, and 'Excelsior' – carmine with a darker central eye.

A well-drained soil which contains lime is suitable for the majority of garden pinks. I find that digging the site over, incorporating just a sprinkling of compost or well-rotted manure in the autumn before planting up-rooted cuttings in the spring, works very well. To help the young plants establish and form side shoots, I nip out the growing point six weeks after planting. A dressing of peat and bone-meal fertiliser plus a dusting of sulphate of potash lightly raked into the soil in March each year helps maintain vigour and flower yield. Cuttings of non-flowering side shoots taken in June to July root in four to six weeks if dibbled into a sandy compost.

Of the modern varieties, 'Doris' with salmon pink flowers, and a sport 'Ruby Doris' are my favourites. Other varieties which have done very well for me include 'Prudence' – pale pink with a darker centre, 'Freckles' – pink flecked red, and 'Diane', salmon pink.

That within a single genus there are so many markedly different races of notable garden plants of ancient lineage is remarkable. For *D. barbatus* – the sweet William – is an old-established favourite which grows wild in southern Europe. In 1535 they were being sold at 3d per bushel, so even at that time they must have been well-known garden plants. To judge from the illustration I have seen, though sweet William have been cultivated for a long time, there has been no dramatic change in the shape or size of the flowers. Annual sweet William are available which flower during July from seed sown under glass in February which is a fairly modern innovation. They grow 6 inches (15 cm) high with flowers a replica in miniature of the more widely grown biennial forms. Sweet William of tradition are usually treated as biennials. The seed is sown in a prepared bed in May, and the seedlings are then large enough for transplanting to their flowering positions in September.

A cross made between sweet William and a garden pink (*D. × allwoodii*) produced a larger, more colourful strain which is marketed under the name 'Sweet Wivelsfield'. All will succeed in good garden soil to which lime has been added, and

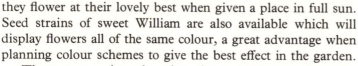

they flower at their lovely best when given a place in full sun. Seed strains of sweet William are also available which will display flowers all of the same colour, a great advantage when planning colour schemes to give the best effect in the garden.

There are species other than those already mentioned as parents of carnations, garden pinks, and sweet William which are well worth a place in rock garden or herbaceous border. They have the advantage of breeding true when raised from seed, and this offers an easy, inexpensive way of adding choice plants to the collection.

D. alpinus from the Austrian Alps forms a hummock of green foliage and blossoms over several weeks from June to August. Individual flowers are large in proportion to the overall size of the cushion, and the colour varies from pink to light purple with a contrasting paler centre. The height of 4 to 6 inches (10 to 15 cm) makes it suitable for growing in the smaller

Top left: *Dianthus seguieri*
Below left: *Dianthus gratianopolitanus*

Dianthus 'Spencer Bickham'

rock garden. Another species that is a very suitable rockplant is *D. seguieri*, which has its home in northern Spain. Other varieties of dianthus which make attractive alpines are 'Spencer Bickham' – with a profusion of pink flowers, and 'Garland' – a good ground cover with pure pink flowers.

D. gratianopolitanus, the Cheddar pink mentioned previously as one parent of the ubiquitous garden pink, is well worth growing on its own merit. When the carpet of glaucous grey-green foliage is embroidered with the fragrant pink flowers during the summer, few plants are more pleasing. A variety known as 'La Bourbrille' is a mirror image of the parent in dwarf form, and it is not too large for a trough garden or table bed. I have had Cheddar pinks in various forms still flowering like young plants after ten years or more.

Though the species *D. chinensis* is not commonly listed in seed catalogues, named varieties derived from it are obtainable.

Of these, 'Heddewigii' shows the intricate markings on the petals which is such a characteristic of the species. 'Fireball' is a useful, double scarlet-flowered form, while 'Baby Doll' with mixed coloured blooms on 6-inch (15-cm) stems offers a prospect for the small garden or window box.

One of the most adaptable dianthus I have grown to date is the maiden pink, *D. deltoides*. The name puzzles me, for there is little I can discover about the plant which suggests the triangle the name implies, unless it is the way each flower-stem divides. I found no problems in my last garden on heavy clay in keeping *D. deltoides* happy, and on the lighter soil in this area of Yorkshire the colonies maintain themselves by self-sown seedlings – a commendable piece of private enterprise. A native of Europe including Great Britain, according to some sources, the height varies depending on location, from between 6 and 12 inches (15 and 30 cm). The narrow leaves are dark green, and the flowers in the best forms are red through to pink. Varieties of *D. deltoides* which offer colour variation are 'Brilliant' – rose,

Above: *Dianthus* 'Alice'

Below: *Dianthus deltoides*

Dianthus 'Daphne'

'Queen of Hearts' – scarlet, and my own choice formed from long acquaintance 'Erectus' – in a glowing, vivid red.

D. pavonius (syn. *D. neglectus*) is curious in my own observation in that it seems happier growing on acid soil rather than one containing lime. To see the short-cropped turf on the alpine pastures near La Grave, pink and red-shaded with the myriad flowers of this lovely dianthus made me desire it for my own rock garden. They make dense tufts of greyish green leaves and in summer large, deep crimson flowers an inch (2.5 cm) or more across, if careful selection is made of plants grown from seed. One characteristic common to all is that the back of each petal is coloured bronze. There are few species more worth raising from seed than this, so that selection can be made of the best colour variations. These can then be propagated by means of cuttings taken in early summer.

In all the books I have read on the subject of dianthus there is one name, that of Montague Allwood, which occurs more frequently than any other, indeed, to British gardeners the pink and Allwood are virtually synonymous. The results of his labours are recorded by the attribution *allwoodii*, but his legacy to gardens extends much further. By introducing the *allwoodii* stock into the breeding lines, a whole new race of perpetual flowering pinks has been established. The first *allwoodii* hybrids were the progeny resulting from a cross between *D. plumarius* and the perpetual flowering carnation. 'Alice', 'Daphne', 'Paul', 'Thomas', and numerous others are a living memorial to his skill as a hybridiser.

In seeking to expand the boundaries of exploration he then crossed *D. × allwoodii* hybrids with dwarf alpine species such as *D. alpinus*, *D. gratianopolitanus* and others to give *D. × allwoodii* 'Alpinus'. This gave plants of dwarf habit with attractive grey foliage and sweetly-scented flowers in a wide range of colours. 'Prince Charming', 'Goblin', 'Little Jock', and 'Fay' all derive in some way from Mr Allwood's first explorations. Many of the modern Show pinks owe parentage, possibly some distance removed to the Allwoodii line.

In addition to the crosses between sweet William (*D. barbatus*) and *D. × allwoodii*, re-crosses were made between the offspring which resulted and other dianthus species. 'Sweet Wivelsfield', 'Delight', and the 'Loveliness' strain with heavily fringed petals combine the best qualities of their parents, plus hybrid vigour which makes them excellent bedding plants. All of them are available in seed form. This offers the easiest method of raising a generous stock for bedding work.

With so many species and garden varieties to work among, dianthus presents a profitable field of exploration to the amateur who wishes to discover some of the excitement and fascination of raising new varieties. At the most it only means a waiting period of two years before the offspring of a cross-pollination between dianthus flowers. Those who do decide to step into the shoes of yesterday's plant breeders should always keep a record of any crosses made. After all, even a dianthus of supreme quality requires a pedigree before it can be registered.

18
Pelargoniums and Geraniums

Geraniums and pelargoniums are so closely akin that at one period in botanical history they were all grouped in one genus. Though the process of cross-pollination to produce new forms of pelargonium has to some extent masked the distinguishing features, they are still revealed by close examination.

The name geranium is derived from the Greek *geranos*, a crane. The members of the genus have regular flowers, the petals of equal size, and the seed pod, as the common name implies, straight – shaped like a crane's-bill. Most are hardy when grown outdoors in the British Isles, being natives of the Northern Hemisphere. All the pelargonium species have irregularly shaped flowers, with two upper petals frequently overlapping and three, often smaller, lower petals. Usually the flowers are spurred, and the seed capsule beaked, splitting into spiral segments when ripe. In spite of the genera having been separate for well over a hundred years, the usual common name for *Pelargonium* is still geranium.

Native to South Africa, Madagascar, Arabia, and similar regions favoured with a warmer climate than our own, it is not surprising that pelargonium species and cultivars are tender, and need heated greenhouse protection in winter if they are to survive. The name is derived from *pelargos* – a stork – the shape of the fruit bearing a fancied resemblance to the bird's beak.

Pelargonium is a large and complicated genus, as anyone who tries to disentangle the species will discover. The confusion was compounded by some botanists in the nineteenth century refusing to accept the division of *Pelargonium* and *Geranium* into separate genera. When the threads of history are sorted out it is the parentage of the regal pelargonium which is the most complex. 'Fringed Aztec', 'Hazel Cherry' and 'Honeywood Lindley' are typical of this group. *Pelargonium × domesticum*, the regal, is derived from crosses between possibly eight species, though I have consulted no authority able to be precise on this point. Of these species, four are especially important. *P. angulosum*, a shrubby species about 3 feet (90 cm) high introduced in the first quarter of the eighteenth century, has purple-carmine flowers which open during the three months August to October. *P. cucullatum*, which arrived about twenty-five years

Above: *Pelargonium cucullatum*,
ancester of the Regal strains,
on the Cape Peninsula

Left:
Pelargonium 'Hazel Cherry' (Regal)
Right:
Pelargonium 'Fringed Aztec' (Regal)

Pelargonium peltatum growing up through a thornbush on a sunbaked hillside in South Africa

before *P. angulosum*, has the same habit, albeit having greater vigour, and the flowers are crimson with deeper veins. The shape and habit is the dominant character contributed by these two. One of the first species to arrive was *P. triste*, brought by one John Tradescant in 1632.

Two species, *P. fulgidum* with petals of bright, fiery red, and *P. grandiflorum*, dwarfer in stature with white flowers, added positively to the wide colour range now seen in the hybrids. Other species which arrived at this time were *P. graveolens* and *P. radens*.

There was promiscuous crossing between the species in the early nineteenth century, and, as with other popular garden plants, hybrid was crossed with hybrid, then back-crossed, until it is a wise pelargonium which knows its own mother, let alone the male parent. Few records were kept of the crosses, so exact pedigrees will never be discovered. But one early hybrid was *P. tricolor*, and it survives today.

P. peltatum, the ivy-leaved geranium, was introduced some time about the year 1700, and has not been subject to the same frenetic intercrossing. Though crosses have been made, these

Below left:
Pelargonium fulgidum flowering in South African scrubland
Below:
Pelargonium 'Duke of Edinburgh' (Ivy-leaved)

Pelargonium tricolor on a stony scree in its native home

Below:
Pelargonium zonale in its wild state in South Africa
Below right:
Pelargonium 'Irene' (Zonal)

have influenced flower colour rather than leaf shape or habit. Modern varieties which are reliable are 'Duke of Edinburgh' and 'L'Elégante'.

The third group, the zonal pelargoniums, *P. × hortorum*, are to most laymen just geraniums or plants with orange-scarlet flowers used by parks departments for summer bedding. Typical varieties of this group are 'Irene', 'Ashfield Monarch' and 'Elizabeth Iris'. The characteristic of this section is the horseshoe mark on the leaf. *P. zonale*, which arrived in the early 1700s, was followed shortly afterwards by the most striking of all the species, *P. inquinans* with brilliant scarlet-coloured, broad-petalled flowers. Crosses between the two species made *Geranium africanum*, as it was then called, a much admired garden flower. Strangely enough the species, *P. zonale*, in spite of the specific name, has not a heavily zoned leaf. More recently other species including the shrubby *P. acetosum*, with long narrow, strap-like rose-coloured petals have been used for cross-pollination to give an even wider range of flower colour and shape.

About one hundred years ago saw the beginning of the

golden age of pelargoniums, when gardeners in private service and local parks began to propagate the zonal or nosegay geraniums for use in massed bedding schemes. The first double was raised in France by the nursery of Lemoine which seems to have specialised in creative hybridisation. Just eighty years ago 'Paul Crampel', the most famous of all pelargoniums, was put on the market. I doubt very much if at the present time any plant has been more widely used for summer bedding. This vivid scarlet pelargonium together with the blue lobelia and the white alyssum brings summer to city gardens throughout the British Isles.

With the advent of the modern F1 hybrid cultivars of pelargonium, unbelievably still listed as geraniums in seed catalogues, a new era has opened. Seed sown under glass in January or February will give flowering-size plants for bedding out during early June, this doing away with the more laborious, time-consuming routine of raising thousands of plants from cuttings each year. For specially effective bedding schemes varieties can be bought which, even when raised from seed, will give flowers all of one colour. 'Mustang', brilliant scarlet, 'Picasso', purplish carmine, and 'Sundance', orange-scarlet, are some of the newcomers which have revolutionised pelargonium cultivation. The dwarf varieties like 'Video' and 'Playboy' are useful for tubs, window boxes, or gardens where there is limited space. The F1 hybrid 'Orange Cascade' has a trailing pendulous growth which is best displayed in hanging baskets or similar positions where a cascade of bloom can be used to good effect. The leaves carry the characteristic zoned markings. However, the zonal pelargoniums offer more than attractively flowered varieties, for there are some available with leaves that are prettily coloured also. The foliage forms (fancy-leaved) are not

Pelargonium 'Picasso'

Pelargonium capitatum on the Cape Peninsula

Pelargonium 'Tuesday's Child'

by any means a modern innovation, for mention is made of painted leaf, or striped, crane's-bills over two hundred years ago. An old hybrid is 'Miss Burdett Coutts', and a more modern variety, 'Tuesday's Child'.

Mr Peter Grieve, a gardener who lived in Bury St Edmunds about 1850, was the first person to take a practical interest in the breeding of variegated or fancy-leaved pelargoniums. In common with most variegated plants, the fancy-leaved varieties require a little more care to grow than those with plain green leaves. Some are bi-coloured with silver or gold banding, others are tri-coloured with red, purple, and other shades added, while 'Red Black Vesuvius', a miniature, has foliage so dark as to be almost black with only a trace of green showing.

The scented-leaved pelargonium became a most popular pot plant, enjoying lodgings in baronial hall and cottage window sill with admirable impartiality. The foliage is so strongly perfumed that just brushing the leaves brings out the distillation. Many are species, others are hybrids principally derived from two species, *P. crispum* and *P. graveolens*. *P. crispum* is an erect-branching shrub, growing 3 feet (90 cm) or more in height, and having a strong citrus scent to its foliage. The cultivar 'Variegatum', with cream and white marbled foliage, is commonly grown. *P. graveolens* hybrids with more deeply divided leaves are known as rose-scented pelargoniums. Another fragrant plant is *P. × fragrans*, smelling of nutmeg, and believed now to be hybrid (*P. exstipulatum × P. odoratissimum*).

Other species with rose-scented leaves include *P. capitatum* with deeply cut leaves and small rose and purple flowers, also *P. denticulatum* with the most fern-like foliage of all. Indeed, so fern-like is the appearance that the tiny whitish flowers come as something of a surprise.

Propagation of all pelargoniums is by seed sown either in January or February in a temperature maintained at about 65°F. (18°C.). Either peat- or loam-based composts are suitable, and the seedlings are transferred to pots when large enough to handle. Cuttings are the means of increase adopted for named varieties. These are made from young growths of 2–3 inches (5 to 8 cm), which can be taken at any time from July to September, and rooted in sandy compost before being potted into John Innes or peat-based compost.

The true *Geranium* is a genus which contains about four hundred species – most of them hardy herbaceous perennials. Most are easily grown decorative plants which will succeed in any reasonable soil. Like so many native plants, crane's-bills blend into the garden landscape, achieving an agreeable harmony which is not always possible with the aggressively coloured pelargonium. That geraniums have been cultivated in our gardens for centuries is faithfully recorded by authors writing in the sixteenth century. Both Gerard and Parkinson list four species as growing in gardens. Gardeners of the time had a poetic knack of choosing pretty, descriptive names for their plants. Who, I wonder, first called *Geranium striatum* 'Queen Anne's Needlework'? The flowers of *G. pratense* were used in Ireland for dyeing wool. On the continent geranium root is mentioned as being used to tan leather, but apart from these two uses, the family figures little in folk lore, though it is occasionally mentioned as a cure for piles and dysentry.

Geraniums vary widely in stature and flower colour over the four hundred species. Some are best accommodated in the rock garden, others are suitable for inclusion in the herbaceous border, while there are some which thrive best in the partially shaded conditions of a shrub border.

G. argenteum, whose leaves are covered in a cobweb of silvered hairs, is one of those lovely plants which, unlike the majority of the clan, is not easy to grow. The flowers are pink but there are selected forms. One I grew called 'Purpureum' had flowers deepening to royal red. The overall height is 6 inches (15 cm), and it grows best in very well-drained soil with full exposure to sunlight. A choice little rock plant well worth persisting with.

Introduced from the Pyrenees in the early 1800s *G. endressii* is altogether more robust and very pretty, a near evergreen which flowers over several months. The form 'Wargrave Pink' has the brightest salmon pink flowers and grows upwards of 18 inches (4 cm) in height. 'Winscomb' has pale mauve flowers.

Also from the Pyrenees, *G. cinereum* is more a plant for the dwarf border or rock garden. A neat hummock of rounded, grey green leaves only 6 inches (15 cm) high with large cupped flowers of pink with darker lines along the veins. The best-known form is *G.c. subcaulescens*, a compact mat of greenery with flowers of rich crimson, each centred with a darker eye. It is a plant which will enjoy being allowed comfortable elbow room along the front of a herbaceous border. A hybrid of this species, 'Ballerina', is exceptional. Its lilac-pink flowers veined

Top:
Pelargonium crispum 'Variegatum'
Above:
Geranium endressii 'Wargrave Pink'

Above and right:
Geranium 'Ballerina'
Below:
Geranium cinereum subcaulescens

with purple open in succession throughout the summer into autumn.

A small species from Albania and Yugoslavia called *G. dalmaticum* offers a different foliage character. The glossy leaves are hard-textured, taking on bright tints before withering in autumn. Flowers in a pleasant shade of pink are carried on 4-inch (10-cm) stems, and all turn neatly outwards to show full face for our appreciation. My plants grow quite happily amongst dwarf shrubs.

So many lovely plants have come from China to grace our gardens that it comes as no surprise to find a choice geranium amongst them. The botanists now insist in the name *G. napuligerum* for this species from the mountains of Kansu in China, but to me it will always be identified by the older, more illustrious name of *G. farreri*. Planted in a free-draining gritty soil, the tufts of grey-green leaves are smothered during early summer with flowers of softest pink, each with contrasting black anthers. The stems are spreading, the overall height about 6 inches (15 cm).

Though I grow *G. ibericum*, this south eastern European is outfaced to such an extent by a hybrid between it and *G. platy-petalum*, that where space is limited I would choose this one, by name *G. × magnificum*. The leaves are deeply divided, turning yellow and pale orange at the onset of autumn. The violet-blue flowers are borne on 24-inch (60-cm) high stems during early summer.

My fondness for *G. macrorrhizum* has not diminished in over twenty years of close acquaintance. Brought from southern Europe over four hundred years ago, this 18-inch (45-cm) high crane's-bill spreads out to make a near weedproof ground cover. It is partially evergreen, but the older leaves die to produce good

Geranium maderense

Geranium × magnificum

Geranium macrorrhizum on the
steep slopes of Mount Olympus

Geranium pratense
'Mrs Kendall Clarke'

autumn colour. The best form, called 'Ingwersen's Variety',
has flowers of rose-pink, whereas those of the type are magenta.
The rounded, light green leaves are pleasantly aromatic to me,
but a friend when visiting the garden described the odour in
derogatory terms as similar to that of a mangy cat. This is
contradicted by the fact that this species is a source for the
distillation of geranium oil. It is an easily grown species which
is at home in most garden soils. An attractive tender species is
G. maderense from Madeira, with purple flowers.

G. phaeum is a western European which is well enough
suited to have escaped from the confines of gardens to become
naturalised. The popular name mourning widow describes the
nodding, reflexed, dark purple flowers to a nicety. The species'
main virtue is that it will make a pleasant light green under-
cover in quite dense shade. In the open, it grows 18 inches (45
cm) high, whereas under shade it tops 24 inches (60 cm).

Native plants which are also beautiful earn a special place
in gardens providing they behave in a respectable, non-invasive
manner. Lovely though the violet blue flowers of *G. pratense*
look in a country landscape, they make themselves too much at
home in the garden by seeding all over the borders. Few have
space or, indeed, the tolerance to accommodate a 3-foot (90-cm)
high crane's-bill which only blooms for three weeks. The best
garden form of the wild crane's-bill is 'Mrs Kendall Clarke'
which flowers throughout June and July.

One of the tallest species I grow at 4 feet (1.2 m) high comes from Armenia, and is identified by the name *G. psilostemon*. Introduced about a hundred years ago, it makes a boskage of elegant, deeply divided leaves, which colour well in the autumn. Succeeding in sun or partial shade, it has vivid magenta crimson, black-centred flowers during the summer.

Plants with attractive foliage afford interest extending way beyond the term granted to the flowers, and *G. renardii* is lovely in leaf, with the white-veined flowers a short term accoutrement. During the whole season sage-green leaves make a 1-foot (30-cm) high dome to complement the more extravagant colours associated with them.

Another geranium which has travelled the years of gardening with me is *G. sanguineum*. The bloody crane's-bill is one of the indispensables – a tough 12-inch (30-cm) high perennial which forms a mat of twiggy stems 18 inches (45 cm) across. The flowers which can be deep magenta through varying shades to mallow pink are a conspicuous feature from early summer. It is one of those trouble-free garden plants, easily propagated simply by pulling away pieces of the sprawling stems with roots attached. A form of this species, *G. sanguineum lancastriense* can be found growing wild on Walney Island off the coast of Lancashire, and has shell-pink flowers pencilled with crimson. I once spent a day on Walney noting all the variations in flower colour amongst the plants growing there. After identifying at least fourteen shades I decided that there is no type colour for this geranium, excellent though it is.

A notable hybrid, good as an edging plant for a wall, is 'Russell Prichard', with crimson-red flowers.

There are some weeds which, even when discovered invading those parts of the garden reserved for choice treasures, do not suffer a summary expulsion. Though a weed and an annual, herb robert, *G. robertianum*, with fern-like foliage and tiny pink flowers, can never be a nuisance. I grow it in amongst the stones which support a bank planted with native flowers, harebells, primroses, and the like.

Wood crane's-bill, *G. sylvaticum*, is described as the northern counterpart of meadow crane's-bill, with me it flowers early when the violet, white-eyed blooms are especially welcome. The leaves are rounded, deeply divided into seven lobes and are a useful weed suppressor. There are pink and white forms to be had for those who search diligently for them.

That a species from the Himalaya should prove a disappointment is sad but, in my experience with *G. wallichianum*, unfortunately true. The flowers are bluish-violet with a white eye, and are so nondescript as not to be worth a place. A seedling which appeared self-sown in the garden in Wales owned by Mr E. C. Buxton more than compensates for the parent's lack of charm. For 'Buxton's Variety' is a thoroughbred, spreading out leafy stems for 18 inches (45 cm) or more, and bearing crop after crop of large saucer-shaped white-centred blue flowers. A lightly shaded corner of the garden preserves the nemophila blue of the flowers.

Geranium sanguineum 'Holden Variety'

Above and below:
Geranium sanguineum lancastriense
at Bressingham Gardens

The species of *Geranium* are not difficult to raise from seed sown into either loam or peat-based composts. Division of the mat-formers also gives the cultivator of geraniums a method of increasing stock. In addition, all those species and varieties I grow will root from cuttings taken in summer.

Amongst my favourite varieties of a much under-rated flower, are:

G. 'Ballerina', an alpine which has dark red veins on each lilac-pink flower.

G. cinereum subcaulescens, an alpine with crimson flowers which last for many weeks.

G. pratense 'Johnson's Blue', which is about 18 inches (45 cm) high, and has attractive light-blue flowers produced in late June, early July.

19
Poppies

There are a great many flowers described in popular terminology as poppies. It is fortunate that botanists demand a more exact definition, or identifying a plant would be very difficult. To the botanist, poppies are those seventy or so species of annual or perennial plants included under the ancient Latin name of *Papaver*. The species are found growing naturally in Europe, northern Africa, western Asia to India. There are two species whose distribution is hard to fit into the general pattern: *Papaver aculeatum*, which occurs in Africa and Australia (a considerable geographical gap), and the other, *P. californicum*, a dainty little annual which to me looks like first cousin to our field poppy, and grows in the United States of America.

Geographical riddles become elementary when confronted with the wealth of myth, lyric, and legend which has grown up to disguise the historical facts of the poppy's evolution in gardening terms. That truth and fiction should be so entwined is not surprising, for the poppy in various forms has been in cultivation for upwards of 2500 years. Controversy begins immediately over the name for the genus *Papaver*. One suggestion, that it derives from the sound made when chewing the seed, suggests a vulgar gluttony, which even a personal experiment in private failed to confirm. The recording of seeds being chewed by no stretch of the imagination suggested *Papaver*, or any other word for that matter. I find Flora Medica offers a more acceptable derivation – linking the name with a Celtic word Papa or pap – the soft baby food in which poppy seeds were mixed to encourage infant slumber.

According to the ancient Greeks the poppy was created by the God of sleep to help Ceres, who was overcome by despair at being unable to recover her daughter abducted by Pluto. Ceres, unable to sleep, was neglecting her duties as the Goddess of crops. After her refreshing, poppy-induced slumber, the corn grew full to harvest. This probably, in some way, explains why *P. rhoeas* – the field poppy or corn rose – was in medieval times considered not to be a weed, but essential in corn fields for the prosperity of the crop. In more recent times, when the field of Waterloo was ploughed after Wellington's victory, the red

Papaver rhoeas growing on the coast of Crete

A Shirley poppy

Papaver somniferum 'Pink Chiffon'

poppies which grew from the newly turned soil were believed to be stained with the blood of soldiers killed in the battle. Thus the superstitions and beliefs contradictorily invest in the same flower symbolic remembrance and the fantasy of grief assuaging sleep. While from Roman times poppies have been offered as memorials to the dead, the Greeks used the flower as proof of sincere love. Young lovers placed a red petal on the palm of one hand, then struck it with the other. Should the petal snap audibly, this proved fidelity, if it failed to break, unfaithfulness. Add the fateful power of prophecy to remembrance and the gift of sleep, and the poppy gains a notable place in garden history. No plant achieves distinction unless it has merit either in economic terms, or as a beautiful addition to the garden – poppies qualify in both these spheres.

Most of the species are hardy, growing successfully in any soils providing the drainage is good, though they give of their lovely best in light, sandy loam, and a place in full sun. Propagation is easy: annual species are grown from seed which is produced in huge quantities. The perennial forms are increased by division of established plants, or in some cases, by root cuttings made in the dormant season. The larger growing perennial species are best accommodated in the mixed or herbaceous border, the annuals which are short term residents can be used to supply bright colour wherever it is needed.

The best known of all poppies, *P. rhoeas*, is familiar to gardeners and non-gardeners because it is found growing wild in fields and odd corners around the countryside. Until recently, one of the prettiest pictures July offered was that of cornfields aflame with scarlet poppies. Modern science, in the shape of selective weed controls, has virtually eliminated the poppy from everywhere except the hedgerows and waste places.

So many of our popular garden flowers owe their success to the single-minded devotion of one person. The stimulus which initially captures their interest varies. With some the love of a particular plant, with others an observation of variation in form or flower colour, while in more prosaic expressions the stimulus may be quite simply economic.

The transformation of corn poppy from weed of the hedgerows to garden plant owes much to the Reverend Wilks of Shirley. Although early in the sixteenth century writers were extolling the beauties of richly-coloured, full double poppies, it was not until the late-nineteenth century that the potential of the corn poppy was appreciated. While he was out walking, Reverend Wilks noticed a wild red poppy which had a white edge to the petals. In due course, he collected seed from this unusual variant and sowed it, no doubt, as most gardeners still do in similar circumstances. He then waited with some impatience for the seedlings to bloom. Selecting only those which showed a variation in flower to bear seed, he discarded all the rest. By selection and re-selection over several years he eventually established the famous Shirley poppy strain which has delighted succeeding generations of gardeners. Although the large, brilliantly coloured, soft-textured flowers last only a short time, new ones are produced in such numbers that blossoming extends over several months. A bed of Shirley poppies in full bloom on a bright August day, in all shades of rose, crimson, pink, and salmon is, indeed, a caprice of summer. The seed may be sown where the plants are to flower, then thinned after germination to 12 to 15 inches (30 to 38 cm) apart. Under normal soil conditions they grow approximately 24 inches (60 cm) high.

Oldest in cultivation, *P. somniferum*, the opium poppy, grows wild in Greece and the Orient. The very large red, purple, pink, or white flowers carried above grey, green leaves followed by the ornamental seed pods, make an imposing picture. The variety 'Pink Chiffon' has double pink flowers and

Below and right: *Papaver somniferum*

is an attractive plant. That this species was originally grown for its edible seeds seems very probable, for I can find no mention of the plant's narcotic properties in early writings on the subject. The seeds do yield a nutty-flavoured, nutritious oil, and this was used instead of olive or almond oil for cooking. Nothing was wasted in the process, as the mash left after expression was fed to cattle or poultry. The seeds mixed with flour and honey were also made into cakes. Apart from being the source of opium which is the principal product of *P. somniferum*, the seed-heads were used to make a sedative in syrup form, and as a hot poultice for external application.

The drug opium is derived from the milky sap which exudes from incisions made in the half-ripe seed capsule. Opium possesses sedative powers, is a valuable medicine, and yields the pain-killing drug known as morphine. When abused, it destroys the health of mind and body.

As a garden plant the species is a beautiful, easily grown hardy annual, popular since the seventeenth century, though

Above and right:
Various colour forms of
Papaver nudicaule,
the Iceland poppy

not universally so, to judge from the name given to the flowers in Elizabethan times – Jack Silverpin, fair without, foul within. To some, the flowers do have an unpleasant smell. In present day seed catalogues there are many varieties on offer, though if Dutch flower paintings depicting the poppy are any guide, this is by no means a modern phenomenon.

The old variety *P. somniferum paeoniaeflorum* with double peony-like flowers is simplified in modern catalogues to peony-flowered, double mixed. Seed sown during April into well-drained sunny corners will in due season yield plants 2½ feet (75 cm) high bearing full double flowers in many and varied colours. To get the best effect the seedlings must be thinned to stand 12 to 15 inches (30 to 38 cm) apart. The old fashioned Latin form *mursellii* has been translated to the easily understood carnation-flowered, which accurately describes the attractively fringed, brightly coloured petals.

P. nudicaule, the Iceland poppy, is native to the arctic regions, and shows marked variations in flower even in the wild

species. Originally introduced during the eighteenth century, Iceland poppies are valuable for garden decoration and as early blooming plants to provide cut flowers. In my experience, they are best treated as biennials under cultivation. Seed is sown where the plants are to flower, then, when the seeds are large enough to handle, singled out at 12 inches (30 cm) apart for smaller growing varieties, or 18 inches (45 cm) apart for taller forms. They will flower the first summer from seed sown under glass in February. Though variations are listed under latinised names in specialist catalogues, the modern seed list offers a whole range of new colour forms. The Kelmscott strain provides a mixture of pastel shades including pink, golden-yellow and orange. The Iceland poppy has a light, elfin quality that contrasts pleasantly with the more statuesque perennials grown in gardens. When required for decoration indoors, the stems should be cut in the early morning just as the buds begin to open. The stalk end can be sealed by dipping the bottom inch or so in boiling water to make the flower stay fresh longer.

The alpine poppy, *P. alpinum*, is familiar to all those who enjoy mountains and the flowers which grow on them. It is a short-lived perennial which, if appearances are any guide, is very closely related to the arctic poppy, though smaller in height and reaching only up to 8 or 10 inches (20 or 25 cm). Seeds scattered along convenient open spaces in rock garden or border are all the introduction the species needs to be made to feel at home. Colour forms do exist, possibly produced from an alliance with *P. nudicaule*, and all are charming in an informal way. Another member of the family which can be grown as an alpine is *P. miyabeanum*. This has attractive yellow flowers and hails from Japan.

P. setigerum is very like the opium poppy in appearance, and is a native of the Mediterranean region. It has deeply cut leaves and violet flowers, and is an annual well worth having, being easy to grow from seed sown direct into the garden. I suspect that many of the cultivated varieties of opium poppy in catalogues, showing hairy divided leaves and purple shaded violet flowers, are the product of cross-pollination between the two closely related species.

Far left: *Papaver alpinum*
in Switzerland
Left: *Papaver miyabeanum*

Below: *Papaver orientale* 'Goliath'

The two most interesting long-lived species for the garden both came from Armenia. Although less widely grown than *P. orientale*, the brightly coloured oriental poppy, *P. lateritium* with orange flowers carried on 18-inch (45-cm) stems in early summer is a species to note. For the small garden its neat compact growth and modest spread are worth considering as an advantage. The oriental poppy, *P. orientale*, has the gift of self-expression, for when carrying a full crop of flowers they are an eye-catching sight. They do need a lot of space to accommodate flower stems which sprawl most indolently, instead of soaring up to display the flowers which can be 10 inches (25 cm) or more in diameter. There is an air of triumphant, albeit garish opulence about the oriental poppy which is hard to ignore. Fortunately, there are cultivars which are

Above:
Papaver orientale 'Black and White'
Left: *Papaver orientale* 'Mrs Perry'
Below: *Meconopsis cambrica*

smaller than the 4 feet (1.2 m) high species which dominated the borders in Victorian gardens. Certainly, they are not particular as to soil, though like all the clan they luxuriate in a free-draining, light loam with a place in full sun. Propagation of new stock is simplicity itself. Young growth cut away with a section of root, or just sections of the fleshy root itself will rapidly establish and grow into vigorous young plants.

Of the well-established cultivars, 'Marcus Perry' is more upright growing than most others, with orange-scarlet flowers on 30-inch (75-cm) stems. Of the same clan, 'Mrs Perry' with salmon pink flowers is slightly dwarfer in stature. 'Goliath' frequently produces leaves on the stems, and I suspect it may be the result of a cross between *P. orientale* and *P. bracteatum*. Its flowers are crimson-scarlet, topping 3-feet (90-cm) high stems. Others which I admire are 'Black and White' with white flowers and a black centre, and low-growing 'Oriana' with ruffled orange flowers.

The layman's definition of poppy covers a broader spectrum than that of the botanist. A good example would be the genus *Meconopsis*, the name roughly translated means poppy-like, which is an apt description of the flower.

The Welsh poppy is our only native species, the rest grow in the Himalayan region, western China, Burma, and northern

Right: *Meconopsis betonicifolia*
Below: *Meconopsis grandis*
(garden cultivar)

India. Though in the poppy family, few *Meconopsis* take kindly to hot dry conditions beloved of the Papaveraceae family. *Meconopsis cambrica*, the Welsh poppy is a perennial which, except in double-flowered forms, seeds so freely as to become a nuisance in the garden. The double variety *M. cambrica florepleno* with yellow or orange flowers, is rather like a miniature Shirley poppy (cultivars of *Papaver rhoeas*) and is a pleasant little perennial.

Best known of the species is the blue Himalayan poppy, *M. betonicifolia*, introduced from western China in 1924. The colour of the flowers, a vibrant sky blue in the best forms, with contrasting yellow stamens, made the plant immediately and deservedly popular. Seed, if sown fresh, germinates with commendable speed when put into lime-free, peat-based compost. Mature plants will also suffer division if this is done just as growth starts in spring. Prepare a bed in lime-free soil with plenty of humus, rotted farm manure, leaf-mould, or peat (all are equally suitable), preferably in a position with light shade from nearby but not overhanging trees. The flowering stems grow up to 4 feet (1.2 m) high.

M. grandis has flowers of vivid blue. The large four-petalled blooms, sometimes more in crown buds, are carried one to a stem in early summer. There are two exceptional forms

Left: *Meconopsis grandis* (Sikkim form)
Above: *Meconopsis integrifolia*

of this most outstanding perennial: one collected by George Sheriff and still sold under the collector's field number G.S.600, and the other called 'Slieve Donard' which came to me from the one-time nursery of that name in Northern Ireland. My plant, which carries a dozen or more very large sky-blue flowers open all at the same time, is a treasure beyond price.

M. quintuplinervia which rambles most happily in peaty soil, produces lavender-blue bells of flowers on 18-inch (45-cm) stems for several weeks during early summer. No plant I have grown sets seed, so recourse must be made to division of the parent, which is easy enough to accomplish in March or April. Reginald Farrer describes seeing the plant on the rolling alps of the Da Tung chain; so beautiful, he says, 'it made the senses ache.' *M. superba* in white makes a happy complement.

Though not a perennial, *M. napaulensis* is so lovely that sowing seed to ensure its continuity in the garden will seem a small price to pay. My plants grow for one or two seasons before sending up a 6- to 8-feet (1.8- to 2.4-m) flowering stem. The colour of petal varies from pink, red, blue, purple, or occasionally white on different plants. They are carried nodding on side branches all up the stem. Another Himalayan species that makes an attractive garden flower is *M. integrifolia*. It has long, pale green, hairy leaves and large yellow flowers.

To overcome the handicap of a name like *Eschscholtzia* and still become popular, a plant would need exceptional qualities. Better known as the Californian poppy, *E. californica* is a charming plant to grow. Beautiful and variable in flower with finely divided grey foliage as a complement, this is a lovely 12 to 24 inch (30 to 60 cm) high annual.

There are many named cultivars in seed catalogues. All thrive when sown into well-drained soil directly where they are to flower. The double-flowered 'Ballerina' and 'Harlequin' hybrids offer a good colour mixture. For the rock garden the 6 inch (15 cm) high yellow-petalled 'Miniature Primrose' is most attractive.

Meconopsis grandis 'Slieve Donard' in the author's garden

Above: *Glaucium flavum* in Greece
Right: *Argemone grandiflora*
in California

Romneya coulteri in southern California

Horned poppy and sea poppy are two popular names for *Glaucium*, natives of Europe and western Asia which are notable for their ornamental foliage and handsome flowers. I have cultivated only one species the horned poppy, *Glaucium flavum*, which grows wild in coastal areas of Britain. A short-lived perennial which reaches 1 to 2 feet (30 to 60 cm) high. The leaves are silver, flowers orange-yellow measuring 2 inches (5 cm) across. There are cultivars with spotted or particoloured petals, though these are not readily available. For me at least, the horned poppy leaves much to be desired as a garden plant.

Usually a plant's popularity can be measured by the number of nicknames it acquires. *Argemone*, another of the Papaveraceae family, has many and to spare: Mexican poppy, prickly bobby, devil's or infernal fig, yellow thistle or argemony – all of which argue that the plant should be better known. Only in hot dry summers do the Mexican poppies smother themselves with an abundance of large flowers. Seed can be sown under glass in March or outdoors in early May. I have grown *Argemone grandiflora* with white blossoms, and the yellow *A. grandiflora lutea*. Both reached 36 inches (90 cm) high and flowered abundantly in the hot, dry summers of 1975 and 1976. Results since then have been less encouraging. *A. mexicana* fared the same. Less upright in growth and when bedecked with bright yellow-orange flowers which give off a rather musky fragrance it excited considerable interest.

Once outside the limits prescribed by the botanists, the list grows beyond controllable numbers, so I will end with the tree poppy, *Romneya coulteri*, a Californian native species and a true perennial. The glaucous stems and deeply-cleft leaves support a succession of large white poppy-like flowers, enhanced with a golden centre of stamens. A warm sunlit place and well-drained soil is to this delightful shrub's taste. Propagation is by suckers, which are freely produced on established plants, or by means of root cuttings taken in November.

20

Heathers

Heather is a collective name used to refer to three different genera of plants which to the layman look very much alike, yet to the botanist are quite separate. The best known in Great Britain, because it occupies such large tracts of land, is *Calluna vulgaris*, the ling or heather of the moors. Though *Calluna* may be the best known of the race, having only one species it is the smallest genus. The name *Calluna* is derived from a Greek word meaning clean – a reference to the use of ling stems for making brooms or besom. Ling grows wild over most of Europe from Norway to Spain, with a last outpost in North Africa.

There are five hundred and more species of *Erica*. No less than four hundred and seventy of these grow naturally in South Africa. Several more of the species inhabit tropical and North Africa, while Europe lays claim to those that remain. Five species are generally accepted as being indigenous to Britain and Ireland.

The third genus is of more manageable size. Saint Dabeoc's heath, Cantabrian heath, or Irish wort, the *Daboecia* of botanists is named after one of Ireland's many saints, St Dabeoc. Linnaeus mis-spelled the rather obscure saint's name by transposing the e and o, so *Dabeocia* became *Daboecia*. Two species and cultivars bred or derived from them are of garden usefulness; they are closely allied to, and need the same soil conditions as *Calluna* and *Erica*.

The ling, *Calluna vulgaris*, has not long been cultivated as a garden plant, only since early in the nineteenth century, if writers of the time are a true guide. Possibly this is explained by the firmly held conviction that ling would not grow when uprooted from the fells which it covers so luxuriantly in the wild.

For those people who farm close to the heather line, life has never been easy. The shallow, acid soil yields no more than a subsistence living, and great use had to be made of any materials lying ready to hand. Heather was pressed into service for roofing; the stems twisted into ropes secured thatch against gale force winds. Serviceable brooms could be fashioned from the stiff, hard stems of this tough little shrub. Indeed, one of the 'wet day' jobs in my early gardening days was making up

Above: *Erica regia* in glorious
colour in South Africa

Left: *Calluna vulgaris*

besoms by lashing heather stems to handles made from coppiced
hazel. A besom is still my first choice as a means of sweeping
clean the lawn.

Highlanders and many north countrymen still consider
that good fortune comes to those who find a patch of white
heather. In even earlier times the Picts made beer from heather.
Unfortunately, the secret manufacturing process was never
divulged to strangers, and so was lost when this most mysterious
race was dispersed. Fresh flowering shoots were used in the
treatment of kidney infections, as an antiseptic, diuretic and
cleansing mixture. In addition, heather contains tannin for
curing leather and a yellow dye for colouring wool. Its use as a
fuel to heat a bread oven, accorded it almost the same high
rating as hawthorn. All things considered, heather was an important constituent of the upland economy. More significantly,

it is an important fodder crop for sheep, deer, and grouse, and is 'farmed' as such by the shepherds of the moors.

Old plants will, in time, grow tall and woody, producing few young shoots suitable for grazing. By burning off sections of the moor each year, the grazier farmers ensure a constant supply of young shoots and a complete rejuvenation of the heather crop. Indeed, tenant farmers in their leasehold since the fifteenth century have agreed to burn off a percentage of the heather on their 'stint' holding annually.

The botanical difference between *Calluna* and *Erica* is easily discovered by looking at the flower. In *Calluna*, the calyx is enlarged and coloured to become the ornamental part of the flower. The *Erica* is traditional in formation having the calyx green and the corolla as the coloured portion. Ling in the language of flowers is a symbol of solitude. Aptly so, for this small yet durable shrub shares its habitat with alpine flowers where human intrusion is the exception. Ling inhabits a terrain which is harsh in climatic terms and not over-rich in plant food. A typical moorland soil consists of acid peat which forms under conditions of high rainfall and a short growing season. Plant debris accumulates quicker than the soil organisms can break it down, and so the partially decomposed material builds up in layers of what we call peat.

In spite of growing under very specialised conditions of soil and climate, *Calluna* will adapt to a wide variety of soils in garden cultivation with one notable exception. I have never seen ling thriving in a lime soil, no matter how much effort and expensive mulching of peat or watering with trace elements was lavished on their cultivation. Given an acid or neutral soil, rich in humus, *C. vulgaris* in all the many forms available, ranging from low-creeping plants to shrubs a metre or more in height, will prove easy to grow. The most suitable soil is one which has

Calluna vulgaris 'Robert Chapman'

Calluna vulgaris 'Alba Rigida'

Calluna vulgaris 'Beoley Gold'
at Bressingham Gardens, Norfolk

been well-prepared with dressings of peat or leaf mould, and is not liable to waterlogging in winter or excessive drying out in summer. *C. vulgaris* flowers in summer and autumn, but varieties are available with coloured foliage, which extends the interest over much of the year.

In an over-rich soil the plants put on vegetative growth at the expense of flowers, so, apart from an annual mulch of peat, any supplementary feeding must be done with care. Annual trimming of the old flower stems will prevent the plants growing leggy and untidy. Done correctly in spring, just before new growths break, they will make well-furnished compact shrubs. A typical ling shoot consists of fresh green-growing tip, then the flowers clustered round the stem, and below the flowers more green foliage. Clipping removes all this shoot including tip and dead flowers just into the green foliage below the old flower stems. Left unpruned, the green tip above the flowers grows ever upwards, while the stem below develops into a 'trunk' devoid of leaves or branches.

Planting is best carried out in the spring in most cases. Make a hole deep enough to accommodate the roots comfortably without constricting them in any way. The finished level should leave the junction between root and stems buried about one inch (2.5 cm) below the soil surface. A mulch of peat after planting will additionally encourage roots to develop from the buried stems, giving an altogether stronger feeding area.

The number of variations from the single species, many of them occurring naturally, is quite remarkable. Of the white flowered varieties, 'Beoley Elegance' with single blooms and 'Alba Rigida' carrying fully double blossoms are useful. 'Beoley Gold' and 'Robert Chapman' are coloured foliaged plants. Of those with double coloured flowers I would choose 'Elsie Purnell', 'H. E. Beale', 'Peter Sparkes', and 'Radnor'.

Though most of the European species of *Erica* were introduced in the last quarter of the eighteenth century, it was not until seeds of two tender South African species arrived in this country that an impetus was given to their popularity. By 1823 over four hundred erica species were in cultivation. The Empress Josephine, an enthusiastic horticulturalist, imported collections of erica from England, although France was at war with Great Britain during that period. These were used to form the basis of a famous heather garden in the grounds of Malmaison. Though beautiful, Cape heaths are not hardy, and it needs considerable skill and experience to grow them well. Nevertheless, royal patronage and the demand created by British gardeners encouraged exploitation of the potential value of the hardy European heaths as garden plants. This worked to such good effect that, although Cape heaths have a limited commercial success for sale as pot plants, the hardy European species enjoy immense popularity as colourful, informal, labour-saving plants.

The hardy species can be grouped under two headings. The tall or 'tree' heaths, which really are the 'giants' of the erica world, grow wild – mainly in Spain, Portugal, and around the Mediterranean. The remaining, and by far the larger group are low growing; five of the species being native to Britain. All of our native plants appear to be lime haters, at least this is my experience. Fortunately, *Erica herbacea* (syn. *E. carnea*), the mountain or Austrian heath from central and southern Europe, is not upset by lime and will grow well in quite alkaline soils. When it was brought to this country in 1763, gardeners grew the newcomer under glass, assuming it to be less than hardy. In fact, *E. herbacea*, the most important species in the genus, ranks amongst the toughest, most resilient shrubs ever to grace our gardens. Flowering as it does from October right through the icy months into early spring, its forms are amongst the most popular of winter flowering shrubs. It is of interest that most of the original work of raising and distributing new varieties was carried out by the nursery firm, Backhouse of York.

Above: *Erica herbacea* 'Myreton Ruby'

Left: *Erica massoni* growing in the South African mountains
Right: *Erica herbacea* 'Springwood White'

The cultivar 'Springwood White', found growing on Monte Corregio in Italy early this century, is a typical example of how so many of the most popular varieties have occurred naturally. One of the best, 'Springwood White' gained an Award of Merit in 1930, followed by an Award of Garden Merit in 1940 from the Royal Horticultural Society. Other excellent varieties selected from the many that are available are 'Eileen Porter', carmine rose – possibly not pure bred *E. herbacea*; 'March Seedling', pale purple; 'King George', deep rose-pink; 'Myreton Ruby', bright red; and 'Vivellii', deep carmine red. Forms having yellow, purple, or bronze foliage are also available, with 'Foxhollow' and 'Anne Sparkes' as possibly the most attractive.

E. cinerea, bell heather, a shrub of 6 to 18 inches (15 to 45 cm) high, enjoys a general distribution over the moors of Britain. Flowering just before the ling, the bright purple, egg-shaped flowers are carried in such profusion that they hide the dark green leaves. Though seemingly adapted to a wide range of soils, bell heather takes more managing in the garden than the redoubtable *E. herbacea*. Given a well-drained, lime-free soil, yet one which holds moisture in a dry summer, bell heather will thrive and put on a brave show throughout the summer to overlap with ling in the autumn.

Amongst the dozens of varieties on offer, some produce flowers in long terminal clusters, others blossom close to the foliage. The stronger-growing, long-stemmed types may be trimmed in much the same way as ling. I delay this pruning until the spring, for the russet-bronze dead blooms are pleasant enough to see on a hoar frosted winter's day. I have one qualification: the 'bells' open at intervals, so both the fresh and dead florets intermingle – not so pleasing as a hearty all-out display. There are numerous colour variations to choose from. Of those with white petals, 'Alba Major' and 'Alba Minor' are noteworthy. The rose-pink 'My Love', and 'Ann Berry' are deservedly popular, while 'Coccinea' is deep ruby red and very compact.

Coloured foliage forms are always interesting. 'Ann Berry', gold in winter, and 'Apricot Charm', light yellow with apricot tints are useful with all the year round leaf tints for the garden.

The cross-leaved heath, *E. tetralix* grows in the wetter moorland hollows, but under garden conditions any soil which does not dry out in summer (so long as it is lime-free) will prove acceptable to this most amiable heath. The flowers open from June to October in dense heads at the tips of the current season's growth. A trim over with shears, followed by a top dressing of moist peat rubbed well down amongst the stems will ensure the shrub's continued good health. The soft-textured foliage is silvery-grey rather than green, and thus makes an attractive feature. 'Alba Mollis', white, 'Hookstone', pink, and 'Con Underwood', crimson purple, are worthwhile additions to a collection.

Above: *Erica tetralix* 'Hookstone'

Left: A heather garden in summer with *Erica herbacea* providing the foliage interest
Right: *Erica cinerea* 'Ann Berry'

E. ciliaris, the Dorset heath, forms a shrub 6 to 15 inches (15 to 38 cm) high that is rather straggly and untidy in general appearance. As would be expected from the popular name, this beautiful native grows wild in the West Country, also in western Ireland and south western Europe. To some extent, the naturally sprawling habit of growth can be corrected by lightly clipping the plants over early in the spring. A lime-free soil and a regular top dressing of peat will suit this species. In my last two gardens, both in Yorkshire, *E. ciliaris* was killed off completely by winter frost one year in three, so it cannot be classified as completely hardy. Flowering from late summer into autumn, it is worth persevering with. Of the white-flowered cultivars, 'David McClintock' is good, but the flowers are pink-tinged at times. 'Corfe Castle' with clear salmon flowers is quite unusual, while 'Maweana', in gardens which offer a kinder climate than mine, with its grey foliage and dark pink blooms is quite lovely.

Left: a beautiful view of
Erica arborea in northern Spain
Right: *Erica arborea alpina* in a
garden setting

Above: *Erica lusitanica* 'George Hunt'
Below: *Erica lusitanica*

Of all the taller growing, or tree heaths, *E. arborea* pleases me the most. In favourable areas it will grow 20 feet (6 m) high, while still retaining a bushy shrub-like habit. The foliage is pale green, carried thickly up the stems. Its white flowers which appear early in March following a mild winter are very fragrant. One would expect a plant native to southern Europe, North Africa and Asia Minor to be so intolerant of conditions in this country as to be not worth growing. Yet in my last garden, two groups of *E. arborea* survived for twenty years, and only showed scorching of the foliage, which necessitated a clip-over with secateurs the following April. These plants were the variety *E.a. alpina* introduced to Kew Gardens at the turn of the century. As it was found growing in Spain on mountain slopes some 5000 feet (1500 m) above sea level, maybe it finds our climate almost congenial.

Erica arborea alpina 'Gold Tips' grew for seven years in my care, then succumbed to the winter of bitter memory 1981–82. Young growths in spring are yellow with just a hint of orange. A sheltered place is essential to the preservation of all *E. arborea*. As with all heathers, cuttings root so readily that any losses can be cheaply and easily made good.

E. lusitanica can grow up to a height of 10 feet (3 m) and spread up to 3 feet (0.9 m). A fairly hardy species, it has pink flower buds and a profusion of white flowers in the springtime. A particularly good garden form is 'George Hunt'. When crossed with *E. arborea*, an attractive shrub with white, scented flowers was produced – *E. × veitchii*. The only known garden form is 'Exeter'.

E. australis, the southern or Spanish tree heath, usually reconciles a tree-like inclination to a shrub reality by growing only 3 or 4 feet (0.9 to 1.2 m) high. A native of Spain and Portugal, it flowers during the spring and on occasions in early summer. Hard frosts kill top growth back to soil level, which is why mature plants are such a rare feature in gardens. The flowers are an attractive shade of red purple, although colours do vary from this to pale pink and white.

Heathers, like other familiar shrubs, have suffered name changes. *E. mediterranea* must now and henceforth, until botanists decree otherwise, be known as *E. erigena*. It is lime-tolerant, growing in cultivation up to 10 feet (3 m), but between 4 and 6 feet (1.2 and 1.8 m) is more usual in northern gardens. The wood of this species is extremely brittle, snow and strong winds breaking whole branches asunder. They do, however, refurbish themselves from soil level if the damaged stems are pruned away. It is native to Spain, south western France, and western Ireland, which is where most of the varieties grown in gardens originate. The rosy-red flowers with a fragrance of sun-warmed honey make a picture to rejoice the eye. The plants I saw on a lough side in Ireland, their flowers a haze of pink against a green and blue landscape, had that ethereal quality which no words can describe. The best-known variety is

Erica × veitchii 'Exeter' in the Savill gardens

Erica australis

Erica erigena 'Brightness'

'Brightness', 24 inches (60 cm) high, with dark foliage and pink flowers. 'W. T. Rackliff' has bright green foliage topped by a profusion of white flowers, and 'Superba' with two-toned flowers of rose-tinted purple. 'Superba' can grow up to 6 feet (1.8 m) high – a most impressive sight when in full bloom on a bright spring day. 'Alba' has delicate white flowers.

Although native to Spain, Corsica, and Italy, *E. terminalis* showed no sign of damage in the twenty years I grew it in a central Yorkshire garden some six hundred feet (180 m) above sea level, but it attained only one third of the 9 feet (2.7 m) recorded elsewhere. The rose-red flowers are developed in clusters at the shoot tips from mid-summer to autumn. It is a quietly pleasant heath which will thrive in acid or alkaline soil. A form with deeper coloured flowers is available.

Possibly my particular regard for the Cornish heath, *E. vagans* stems from the fact that my first heather garden was made on heart-breakingly heavy clay soil, and this species thrived and flourished better than any others I planted. Native to Cornwall, France, Spain, and locally in Ireland, this species grows in the wild up to 30 inches (75 cm) and has rather washed-out flowers of pale pinkish purple from mid-summer to October. Garden forms include much improved varieties, which are neatly compact in growth with brightly coloured flowers. The white 'Lyonesse', bright rose 'St Keverne', and darker cerise-red 'Mrs D. F. Maxwell' together with the attractive foliage of 'Valerie Proudley' are first class beginnings to a collection. Given regular dressings of peat, they will grow tolerably well in limy soil.

With the increasing interest in heathers as decorative plants, efforts to supply new varieties by cross-pollination between related species was inevitable. Some of the earliest hybrids, however, came from chance cross-pollination which occurred when two different *Erica* species were grown alongside each other in a nursery garden. *E. × darleyensis*, which appeared some hundred years ago in a Derbyshire nursery, is the product of natural cross-pollination between *E. herbacea* (syn. *E. carnea*) and *E. erigena*. Stronger growing than *E. herbacea* but with the same long flowering season combined with *E. erigena*'s free blossoming character, the chance seedlings are a valuable addition to the range. Starting to flower in December and continuing until May, they span the bleakest months of the year:
'Arthur Johnson' with mauve pink flowers in long spikes,
'Darley Dale' the original hybrid with lilac rose blossom,
'George Rendall' lilac pink, and the white flowered
'Molten Silver' ('Silverschmelze') are good value.
'J. W. Porter' has attractive mauve-pink flowers.

Daboecia contains only two species and is quite different in appearance to the other heathers. As with *Calluna* and most *Erica* species, a lime-free soil is essential for their well-being. The individual egg-shaped flowers are large by comparison with those of the other heathers, appearing from late summer to early autumn. Once the flower 'sets' (is fertilised), the corolla drops and the dead stems can be trimmed away – a summary pruning which keeps the bush compact.

Daboecia azorica from the Azores was introduced in 1929, so it is still very much a newcomer. The deep red flowers hang pendant on stalks from the 4- to 6-inch (10- to 15-cm) high stems. The average height varies, depending on variety, between 10 and 12 inches (25 and 30 cm). *D. cantabrica* is, I think, of better constitution, certainly hardier than *D. azorica*, and taller growing – up to 18 inches (45 cm) or even more. The rosy purple flowers which are displayed from June to late October are carried on long, leafless stems, well clear of the dark green leaves. *D. cantabrica* is a native of Ireland and western Europe. A light loam with a generous admixture of peat, plus a clip over in spring to remove the spent flower stems and the tips of the previous seasons growth, is all the attention this attractive dwarf shrub requires. Cultivars of the recently introduced hybrid, *D. × scotica*, combine hardiness with compact growth.

Of all the varieties *D. cantabrica alba* is my favourite. The vivid green leaves supply a proper contrast to the large, pure white floral bells. 'Hookstone Purple' with purple flowers, and 'Praegerae' with salmon-pink bells are very fine dwarf shrubs, and the latter exceptionally so.

Left: *Erica vagans* 'Valerie Proudley'
Right: *Daboecia cantabrica* 'Praegerae'

Propagation of *Calluna*, *Erica*, and *Daboecia* is easily achieved either by means of cuttings or layering. Non-flowering shoots of the current season's growth taken in the season June to October are suitable. Equal parts of fine-grade sphagnum moss, peat and sharp lime-free sand or crushed granite make a good cutting compost. Unless large quantities of cuttings are required, dibble the cuttings into a 6-inch (15-cm) pot of the above compost, then plunge the container into a frame. Water only with lime-free water as required, and rooting should take place in 6 weeks or a little longer according to the season. Those taken in October may not be well-enough rooted for potting off until the following spring.

Layering is the fool-proof method. Selected plants growing in the garden need only be mounded up with the peat-sand mixture, so that the base of the stems are covered. Sufficient roots have usually formed after 6 to 8 months for the layer to be removed. Better results are gained by pegging down selected branches into compost with pegs made from heavy duty galvanised wire.

A heather border makes a pleasant, labour-saving feature. By careful choice from the varieties on offer of *Daboecia*, *Erica*, and *Calluna* it is possible to have plants to bloom for all the twelve months in the year. Maintenance is minimal, for apart from clipping and mulching, the weeding is reduced by the living ground cover of heather foliate.

Left: *Erica × darleyensis* 'J. W. Porter'

Index